REAL ESTATE PROFESSIONALS

PRACTICAL CAREER GUIDES

Series Editor: Kezia Endsley

REAL ESTATE PROFESSIONALS

A Practical Career Guide

TRACY BROWN HAMILTON

ROWMAN & LITTLEFIELD

Lanham • Boulder • New York • London

Published by Rowman & Littlefield
An imprint of The Rowman & Littlefield Publishing Group, Inc.
4501 Forbes Boulevard, Suite 200, Lanham, Maryland 20706
www.rowman.com

86-90 Paul Street, London EC2A 4NE, United Kingdom

British Library Cataloguing in Publication Information Available

Library of Congress Cataloging-in-Publication Data

Names: Hamilton, Tracy Brown, author.
Title: Real estate professionals : a practical career guide / Tracy Brown Hamilton.
Description: Lanham : Rowman & Littlefield, [2022] | Series: Practical career guides | Includes bibliographical references. | Summary: "Real Estate Professionals: A Practical Career Guide covers the steps you need to take have a career in this field and includes interviews with professionals currently working in this field"—Provided by publisher.
Identifiers: LCCN 2022020122 (print) | LCCN 2022020123 (ebook) | ISBN 9781538170335 (paperback) | ISBN 9781538170342 (epub)
Subjects: LCSH: Real estate business. | Real estate business--Management. | Real estate agents. | New business enterprises.
Classification: LCC HD1375 .H36 2022 (print) | LCC HD1375 (ebook) | DDC 333.33.068—dc23/eng/20220707
LC record available at https://lccn.loc.gov/2022020122
LC ebook record available at https://lccn.loc.gov/2022020123

Contents

Introduction

So You Want a Career in Real Estate

*W*elcome to the world of real estate! That you have made the choice to pick up this book and read it means you are taking a first step in pursuing your career goal in an exciting, ever-evolving, and growing field, and to working as a real estate agent or broker to help clients buy, sell, and rent properties. Whether you already know exactly what kind of job you want or you are simply looking for more information about the real estate profession to see if it's something for you, this book will inform you about what real estate jobs exist and entail and what steps you can start taking now, no matter where you are in your educational path, to get started with pursuing your goals.

If you're thinking about a career in real estate, either as a full-time venture or as a side gig, you are definitely not alone. Each month, according to 2020 statistics, about seventeen people in the US alone google "how to become a real estate agent," and about two million people hold active real estate licenses.[1] There's a reason so many find a career in real estate attractive: the job can be flexible and you can be your own boss. You get to meet a lot of people and have the satisfaction of helping them to buy their dream home or secure the ideal business property. There are a lot of perks.

And the real estate profession is a healthy one: according to the Bureau of Labor Statistics, the number of real estate agent and broker jobs is projected to increase by 4 percent between 2020 and 2030—this is slightly slower growth than other professions, but it's still showing growth, and there were more than five hundred thousand real estate jobs in the US in 2020.[2]

This book will focus on real estate agent and real estate broker careers. While the jobs are similar, there are some differences, which the book will cover in more detail later on. In a nutshell, real estate agents are licensed to help people buy, sell, and rent real estate properties such as apartments, homes, and office buildings. Brokers are real estate agents who have completed additional training and licensing requirements. They can work independently and hire other real estate agents to work for them.

The life of a real estate professional typically involves the following:

- Reviewing listings for suitable properties and seeking new clients to serve
- Performing administrative work in the office
- Arranging and conducting meetings with clients, including scheduling appraisals and inspections
- Staging and showing homes
- Generating leads for available properties, researching, marketing, and accompanying clients to property closings

This book is the ideal start for understanding the various careers available to you within the real estate field, which one is right for you, and what path you should follow to ensure you have all the training, education, and experience needed to succeed in your future career goals—as well as advice on how to make contacts, secure leads, and sell properties.

Whether you want to commit yourself full-time to a career as an agent or broker or you envision working in real estate as a side job—and whether you want to work for a large agency or give real estate a go on your own—this book will help you understand how to begin now, whether you are a high school student or a university graduate, to set yourself on the course to a successful career in real estate.

A Career as a Real Estate Agent or Broker

Real estate is a broad field. Many various—and varied—professional input goes into the buying, selling, and renting of properties, including financial and legal experts, marketing and sales professionals, and administrative support. This book will primarily focus on the jobs of real estate agent and broker, but there will be mention of other jobs within the field, especially those that work closely with agent or broker in the real estate transaction process. The following are types of jobs available within the real estate arena:

Real estate agents help clients buy and sell properties, as well as rent or rent out properties.

Real estate brokers are responsible for negotiations between buyer and seller parties and for arranging real estate transactions.

Real estate property managers take care of a property, both financially and in terms of maintenance, and see to the needs of any tenants living or working there.

Real estate transaction coordinators serve as liaisons between the client, real estate agent, escrow company, and mortgage brokers.

Showing assistants assist agents by presenting a property to clients and telling them all about it.

Real estate marketing specialists create marketing content, manage social media, develop printed materials, create digital content, prepare campaign emails, and manage the brand as a whole for real estate agencies.

Real estate appraisers estimate the value of the property before the property is sold, taxed, mortgaged, or insured. This requires additional licensure.

The Market Today

Every field you can imagine feels itself in a bit of uncertainty right now. A financial crisis, a global pandemic—events beyond our control—can cause insecurity and changes in the most stable of professions. Real estate has not escaped this reality, yet it is a profession where growth is still expected in the coming years, despite the challenges we've all experienced.

And, like other jobs, automation—the replacement of human beings with technologies such as artificial intelligence (AI)—poses a threat to real estate jobs. According to UpNest, "Here's the percentage likelihood these real estate jobs will be automated in the near future":

- 97% Real Estate Brokers
- 99% Telemarketers
- 98% Loan Officers
- 86% Real Estate Sales Agents[3]

But do not despair. As with other careers, technology advances may *change* how the real estate job is done, but they won't destroy our need for talented agents and brokers. There will always be a demand for property and for the people who help make property ownership possible. Although tasks like property searches are already automated, some aspects of the job are for now best left to human hands, including, according to UpNest:

- Professional negotiations
- Creating property descriptions that sell
- Crafting contracts which really protect buyers and sellers
- Keeping transactions together when issues and disagreements arise
- Making sense of all the data
- Acting as a buffer to protect seller privacy[4]

Becoming a real estate professional gives you the opportunity to play a big role in helping people realize the dream of owning their own property, through helping them navigate the sometimes complicated process of finding and purchasing real estate. *Feverpitched/iStock/Getty Images.*

What Does This Book Cover?

This book covers the following for careers in real estate, as an agent or broker, freelancer or full-timer, self-employed or working for an agency:

- Understanding what real estate agents and brokers do and what characteristics many who land in these fields possess
- How to form a career plan—starting now, wherever you are in your education—and how to start taking the steps that will best lead to success
- Educational requirements and opportunities and how to fulfill them
- Tips on writing your résumé, interviewing, networking, and applying for jobs
- Resources for further information

Where Do You Start?

No matter where you are in your education, from junior high to college graduate and beyond, it is never too soon to get started pursuing a career in real estate. Even though you have to be eighteen to officially start working in the field, you can begin developing the skills you will need right now.

Math skills, business skills, interpersonal skills—these will all be important for you as a successful real estate professional. Developing an interest in property, following changes in the market, understanding how mortgages work—these are also valuable ways to increase your odds of achieving your goals in a competitive, exciting field.

Once you've read this book, you will be well on your way to understanding what kind of career you want, what you can expect from it, and how to go about planning and beginning your path. Let's get started.

Why Choose a Career as a Real Estate Professional?

*A*re you someone who is always observant of the layout of apartments and homes you visit? Are you attuned to changes in neighborhoods or how public spaces or buildings are utilized? Do you love to help people find solutions to their problems, and do you feel good when you can assist someone in finding just what they are looking for? There are many reasons why a career in real estate appeals to people—these are just a few.

People who are drawn to real estate careers have a good sense of business and market value and are self-starters who have the drive to work hard and become successful entrepreneurial-minded professionals. Many real estate agents and brokers are self-employed, which makes the job flexible to fit your other life obligations or goals and help you achieve that work/life balance that is increasingly recognized as key to your health and happiness.

Another point: real estate careers do not require years and years of studying and thousands invested in multiple university degrees to achieve. This is not at all to say that anyone can do it—there are qualifications that you will have to earn, which we will discuss, and lots of additional knowledge you'll want to hone to achieve your career goals, such as business and marketing skills. But it does mean that if you decide to launch a career in real estate, you can hit the ground running in a relatively short period of time—and start bringing in income, which is also not a bad thing.

The fact that you are reading this book indicates you, too, are considering real estate as a career. Choosing a career is a difficult task, but as we discuss in more detail in chapter 2, there are many methods and means of support to help you refine your career goal and home in on a profession that will be satisfying and will fit you and your natural characteristics and interests the best.

Of course, the first step is understanding what a particular field—in this case real estate—actually encompasses and informing yourself of the future outlook of the profession. That is the emphasis of this chapter, which looks at defining the field in general and then more specific terms, as well as examining the past and predicted future of the field.

So as with any career, there are pros and cons, which we will discuss in the chapter. In balancing the good points and less attractive points of a career, you must ask yourself whether, in the end, the positives outweigh any negatives you may discover. This chapter will also help you decide whether a career in real estate is actually the right choice for you. And if you decide it is, the next chapter will further offer suggestions for how to prepare your career path, including questions to ask yourself and resources to help you determine more specifically what kind of career related to real estate suits you the very best.

What Is the Real Estate Industry?

The real estate industry refers to the business of selling, renting, and managing real estate, of which there are several types. When people refer to "real estate," they mostly think of buildings, particularly homes or apartments where people live. But there are other types of real estate, each with their own function and purpose, all of which are owned, rented, or managed.

> **Note:** Each state has its own requirements you must meet to work in real estate as an agent or broker, and most often many of these requirements apply to property managers as well. States usually have requirements regarding (but not limited to) age, education level (usually high school or equivalent), pre- and postlicensing, background checks, some level of continuing education, reporting of any criminal history, and what requirements there are to achieve the next level of licensing.

The main types of real estate—and the ones that are the focus of this book—are:

Land. Land is often not thought of as real estate because it mostly is not valued for any buildings or structures, but for the space itself. It is the starting point for all types of real property. Developers purchase land with plans to use it for a specific, designed purpose, such as an office park or housing area.

Residential. Residential real estate is something we are all familiar with: the structures in which people live. This can mean single-family homes, apartments, condominiums, townhouses, and other types of living spaces.

Commercial. Commercial property refers to land and buildings that are used by businesses to carry out their operations. Examples include shopping malls, individual stores, office buildings, parking lots, medical centers, and hotels.

Industrial. Industrial real estate is a type of property used by businesses for activities such as factory work, mechanical productions, research and development, construction, transportation, logistics, and warehousing.

REAL ESTATE AGENTS

Real estate agents are the people who work directly with clients to buy, sell, or rent properties. They help clients find or advertise properties for sale or rent and work with them throughout the process of negotiating prices and contracts. Here are some estimates for real estate agents, according to the Bureau of Labor Statistics:

- Hourly pay: $24.63
- Annual wage: $51,220
- Projected growth (2020–2030): 4 percent[1]

Note: We will discuss the difference between an agent and a broker elsewhere in the book, but one thing to note is that as an agent you must pay a fee to join a real estate brokerage to work under. This can cost between $25 and $500 and upward per month, depending on the brokerage and your area.

REAL ESTATE BROKERS

A real estate broker can work for a company—called a brokerage firm—that employs a team of real estate agents who help facilitate a transaction between the buyers and sellers of property. A broker works for—or represents—either the buyer or seller in the transaction to ensure that their party achieves the best possible deal or terms in the agreement. Here are some estimates for real estate brokers, according to the Bureau of Labor Statistics:

- Hourly pay: $24.63
- Annual wage: $51,220
- Projected growth (2020–2030): 4 percent[2]

REAL ESTATE/SHOWING ASSISTANTS

As the name implies, a real estate or showing assistant works to support the agent in working with clients—buyers or sellers, rentees or renters—and showing them properties. This can include visiting properties with clients and being prepared to give accurate information about the property, as well as ensuring that it is clean and otherwise presentable for optimal viewing. Here are some estimates for showing assistants, according to Salary.com and the Bureau of Labor Statistics:

- Hourly pay: Not listed
- Annual wage: $30,880[3]
- Projected growth (2020–2030): 4 percent[4]

PROPERTY MANAGERS

Property management firms help real estate owners rent out the units in their buildings. They are responsible for tasks such as collecting rent, showing units to potential renters, fixing deficiencies, doing repairs, and managing tenants. They typically earn a percentage of the rent from the property owners they work for. Here are some estimates for property managers, according to the Bureau of Labor Statistics:

- Hourly pay: $28.68
- Annual wage: $59,660
- Projected growth (2020–2030): 3 percent[5]

> **Note:** As mentioned earlier, there are other roles in the real estate industry that an agent or broker or property manager will encounter and work together with during a transaction; however, this book will primarily focus on careers as an agent or broker. Other careers worth taking a deeper look into, if you are interested, include real estate sales and marketing, real estate lending, professional services such as legal or accounting services, and real estate developers.

Lots of people are involved in the buying, selling, and renting of a property, be it residential, commercial, or industrial—or even land that does not yet have property on it. Real estate professionals therefore serve a very important function in society. *courtneyk/E +/Getty Images.*

Types of Residential Real Estate

Even within the residential category, depending on where you live and the clients you serve, there are all sorts of residential properties you may be dealing in. The following are "some specific examples of different types of real property," outlined by the Corporate Finance Institute:

- **Single-family dwelling**—Any home designed for only one family
- **Multi-family dwelling**—Any group of homes designed for more than one family
- **Attached**—Any unit that's connected to another (not freestanding)
- **Apartment**—An individual unit in a multi-unit building. The boundaries of the apartment are generally defined by a perimeter of locked or lockable doors. Often seen in multi-story apartment buildings.
- **Multi-family house**—Often seen in multi-story detached buildings, where each floor is a separate apartment or unit
- **Condominium (condo)**—A building with individual units owned by individual people
- **Detached house**—A free-standing building not connecting to anything else (a stereotypical "home")[6]

The Pros and Cons of Real Estate Careers

As with any career, one in real estate carries with it upsides and downsides. But also true is that one person's "pro" is another person's "con." If you consider yourself a strong "people person" who has the enthusiasm and ambition to make a good sale, you will likely thrive as a real estate agent. If you seek a nine-to-five position working with the same people in teams day in and day out, you will maybe get less enjoyment out of working with a constantly changing flow of new clients. There are lots of aspects to consider when choosing the right career for you.

Tip: Although it's one thing to read about the pros and cons of a particular career, the best way to really get a feel for what a typical day is like on the job and to see the challenges and rewards is to talk to someone who is already working in the profession, or who has in the past.

Although there are too many aspects of a real estate profession to list, and it's unlikely that a person will find them all good or all bad even if we did, there are some generalizations that can be made when it comes to what is most challenging about the job and most gratifying that you should consider. Here are some general pros:

- You will have the flexibility to, for the most part, set your own schedule and determine how many overall hours you want to work.
- There is no salary cap on how much you can earn as a real estate agent. The stronger your drive and business savvy, and of course the more hours you work, the stronger the potential of earning more.
- You will have a job with a strong feel-good factor that stems from helping people achieve a major life milestone, whether it be purchasing the perfect home or acquiring the perfect business location.
- It is a constantly evolving field with new trends and innovations and an endless opportunity for learning.
- Although you will definitely spend time behind a desk doing administrative tasks, you will also be able to work "in the field," visiting properties and meeting with clients, and you will work with and for lots of different people with all kinds of personalities and interests.

And here are some general cons:

- While the flexibility of your hours can be a major draw to a career in real estate, without proper organization and discipline and without clear boundaries imposed by a more traditional job, you may find yourself working far more hours than you would otherwise.
- As with any self-employment career, there is no safety net if the market takes a downturn and your business slows down or stalls for periods of time. You have to be very careful financially about saving for a rainy day.
- It is a high-pressure field that requires an ability to manage stress well as well as to multitask. Sales may look easy from the outside, but it takes continuous hard work and drive to succeed in this field.
- While you will meet a lot of people in your work, most of the people you will engage with as customers of yours will be involved in onetime transitions—so you won't have the traditional continuity of people you work alongside.

"By meeting so many people, both agents and consumers, you get to learn all types of perspectives and cultures. You hone your communication skills as a result. This, in turn, makes you calm when you are dealing with all aspects of your life, professional and personal."—Janis DeVito, real estate broker

What Is a Real Estate License, and How Do I Get One?

A real estate license is a requirement for working as a real estate agent or broker, and sometimes for property managers as well. Taking a professional role in a real estate transaction requires you to know and follow specific rules, laws, and procedures, and passing a license test to earn your license shows you have the required qualifications.

But there is no national, US-wide license: you will need to pass the test and earn the license in the state in which you plan to work. Some states have so-called reciprocal licensing agreements with other states, which means you can get your license in one state and use it in another without having to take an additional license examination.

To prepare for the test, you have to fulfill your state's prelicensing require-ment before you sit for the exam. This means completing a set number of hours of coursework, in a classroom or online, which is determined by your state's own rules. In California, for example, a candidate for the real estate license test must complete three real estate classes that total 135 hours, whereas in Florida, you are required just 63 hours of coursework. Check the rules in your state to find out what your prelicense requirements are. Estimated costs for the course-work, regardless of your state, are approximately $350.

The exam itself will cost you an additional amount, anywhere from $100 to $300. The exam is in multiple-choice format. The computerized test is split into two parts: a national portion on general real estate principles and practices, and a state-specific section that covers your state's real estate laws. You can find practice exams online to get an idea of the types of questions you will be asked. Check out test-guide.com for free real estate practice exams, for example.

Once you have passed the test—and you need to pass both parts—you are nearly there, but not quite. You must then submit an application to activate your license. This comes with another fee, this time of around $200–$400. So you definitely want to be serious about a career in real estate before you invest the time and money involved in acquiring your license.

Note: Many assume a real estate agent is the same as a Realtor, and it's mostly true—the jobs are very much the same, except to be a Realtor you must belong to the National Association of Realtors and adhere to a strict code of ethics. The association is the largest trade association in the US, with more than 1.3 million members including salespeople, brokers, property managers, appraisers, counselors, and other professionals in the residential and commercial real estate industry. It's a privilege you'll have to pay about $185 for, but this gives you access to perks such as business tools, market data and research, professional development opportunities, and other discount programs to help give you an edge in business.

How Healthy Is the Job Market for Real Estate Professionals?

The real estate job market is an interesting and overall healthy one. The industry has waves of ups and downs, which you've likely read or heard about at times in the news. As with all industries, the pandemic has had an impact on real estate. The number of home sales increased in 2020—surpassing 2007 (pre–financial crisis) levels.[7]

Note: One thing you will be very familiar with as a real estate professional is a mortgage. Although you will not personally be involved in arranging the actual finances of a real estate property you work with a client to buy or sell, whoever is buying will have to secure the money to make the purchase. Because property is so expensive—as compared with, say, buying a pair of shoes—it is unusual to buy a property outright. All property buyers must therefore arrange with a bank a mortgage, which is a contracted loan. Basically, a person borrows the money they need for their home or business property or land, and the bank agrees to loan it with the real estate being purchased as security for the money lent. The mortgage is the agreement between the lender (the bank) and the borrower (the party buying the real estate).

Growing demands for homes across the country has made prices rise, creating a good situation for sellers but a difficult one for buyers. While affordability concerns continue to grow, low mortgage rates, increased savings, and a strengthening job market have all increased the number of potential buyers in the market—which is good news for real estate professionals.

The real estate industry has its ups and downs, but real estate will almost certainly always be a viable career path. People will continue to need places to live and work. *Drazen Zigic/iStock/Getty Images.*

What Is a Median Income?

Throughout your job search, you might hear the term "median income" used. What does it mean? Some people believe it's the same thing as "average income," but that's not correct. While the median income and average income might sometimes be similar, they are calculated in different ways.

The true definition of median income is the income at which half of the workers earn more than that income, and the other half of workers earn less. If this is complicated, think of it this way: Suppose there are five employees in a company, each with varying skills and experience. Here are their salaries:

- $42,500
- $48,250
- $51,600
- $63,120
- $86,325

What is the median income? In this case, the median income is $51,600, because of the five total positions listed, it is in the middle. Two salaries are higher than $51,600, and two are lower. The "average income" is simply the total of all salaries, divided by the number of total employees. In this case, the average income is $58,359.

Why does this matter? The median income is a more accurate way to measure the various incomes in a set because it's less likely to be influenced by extremely high or low numbers in the total group of salaries. For example, in our example of five incomes, the highest income ($86,325) is much higher than the other incomes, and therefore it makes the average income ($58,359) well higher than most incomes in the group. Therefore, if you base your income expectations on the average, you'll likely be disappointed to eventually learn that most incomes are below it.

But if you look at median income, you'll always know that half the people are above it and half are below it. That way, depending on your level of experience and training, you'll have a better estimate of where you'll end up on the salary spectrum.

Am I Right for a Real Estate Career?

So is the real estate industry the right career choice for you? This is a tough question to answer, because really, the answer can only come from you. But don't despair: there are plenty of resources both online and elsewhere that can help you find the answer by guiding you through the types of questions and considerations that will help you understand the requirements of a particular job and what characteristics and commitments are required to succeed in it. Examples of these are covered in more detail in chapter 2.

For now, let's take a look at the general demands and responsibilities of a real estate career—as were mentioned previously in the section on pros and cons—and suggest some questions that may help you discover whether such a profession is a good match for your personality, your interests, and the general lifestyle you want to keep in the future.

And if you aren't sure where you want to live, for example, or whether you will have a family of your own or change your mind about your career path later, that's fine too. Just take time to ensure you are making a choice that feels right for you right now, and certainly be wary of any red flags you notice when considering a career path.

Although there is not one "type" that matches the profile of a successful real estate professional, there are some aspects of the job that you can anticipate and think about whether it sounds like something you would naturally enjoy or expect to struggle with.

Note: Of course, no job is going to match your personality or fit your every desire, especially when you are just starting out. There are, however, some aspects to a job that may be so unappealing or simply mismatched that you may decide to opt for something else, or equally you may be so drawn to a feature of a job that any downsides are not that important.

One way to see if you may be cut out for a career in real estate is to ask yourself the following questions:

Do I genuinely care about other people, and can I form trusting relationships? Clients really will need to feel a "click" with you, to trust you entirely and to feel that you genuinely understand and will advocate for their wishes. Real estate transactions can feel very high stakes for people—they are making an important decision and need to know their agent or broker is a reliable expert who is on their side.

Do I love good challenges and find innovative ways to rise to them? Am I a creative go-getter who will tirelessly work toward my goal, without guarantees of success? In other words, are you ready to accept the challenge of running your own business and being your own boss? Can you accept responsibility if something goes wrong with a sale or a client? Are you prepared to take the financial risks of not having a guaranteed salary?

Am I naturally inquisitive, and do I know how to ask the right questions to lead to deeper understanding of an issue? A natural curiosity and excellent listening skills are paramount to an effective real estate agent's success. A talent for seeking out new opportunities and clients, for learning new information about development plans or neighborhoods, and a curiosity to learn as much as you can about all aspects of the business will be strong assets in your career.

Am I tolerant and nonjudgmental? Can I get along with all personality types? You will have to work with a range of people and personalities, and because any sales situation can be stressful (people may feel vulnerable or combative), you will have to be able to maintain a professional attitude and demeanor and not present any bias in the job. Your interpersonal communication skills need to be exceptional when interacting with clients and their families in order to have effective and open discussions about the issues at hand and the approach being taken.

Do I have an overly excited attention to detail and an inability to leave any stone unturned? Do you give up easily, or do you have the fortitude to keep probing, keep thinking, keep searching for new answers and approaches? You may be dealing with clients who have circumstances from financial to health related that make their real estate dealings more challenging. They'll need a tireless fighter in their corner.

At the same time, can I function under pressure? Sales of any kind is not the kind of profession that enables you to shut down your computer at 5:00 p.m. and go home and think about something else until the next morning. Real estate professionals are susceptible to taking their work home with them, to being available at all hours. To avoid burnout, it is important to have strategies to deal with this kind of pressure as well as the emotional drain of thinking deeply about other people's struggles.

DOING SOMETHING I LOVE, AND BEING SUCCESSFUL AT IT

Laura Soride. *Courtesy of Laura Soride.*

Laura Soride became a licensed Realtor in 2006 and obtained her broker's license in 2008. She started the Laura Soride Team in 2012 and, in 2014, took over ownership of the local RE/MAX Affiliates office. Laura is constantly signing up for real estate–related classes to further her expertise in real estate: she has obtained eleven designations (certified new home sales professional; military resource professional; certified negotiation expert; At Home with Diversity [AHWD] certification; short sale & foreclosure certification; accredited buyers representative; e-PRO technology certified agent; CRS [certified residential specialist]; C2EX [Commitment to Excellence], National Association of Realtors; SHC [smart home certification]; pricing strategic advisor certification) and is currently studying for more.

How did you choose real estate as a career?

I purchased my first home at the age of eighteen and later remodeled my childhood home. I felt great pride in home ownership and wanted to help others achieve the same goal. My first job was as a cosmetologist, and I loved working with the public. I had studied Spanish and Japanese languages throughout high school and college and thought all of that combined education would be put to good use in real estate.

Can you describe your educational background and career path to date?

After graduating from high school, I attended a cosmetology college. Once I graduated with my cosmetology license, I started attending a local community college part-time while working full-time at a hair salon. I eventually obtained my liberal arts degree and then attended the University of Iowa to study Japanese. I was also able to study abroad in Japan and graduated with a major in international studies, a minor in Asian languages and literature (Japanese language), and a certification in international business. Definitely more education than is required to be a Realtor!

What is a typical day on the job for you?

No two days are ever the same in real estate! I am committed to being at my office full-time if I am not on showings or listing appointments with clients. I'm often at closings, working on mailings, updating my client database, sending personal notes to clients, attending continuing education, etc. Early in my career I enjoyed being in the office around others and learning from their experiences. I definitely don't feel as productive working from home.

What's the best or most satisfying part of your job?

Knowing that I gave my clients the best service possible, having them trust my abilities and referring me to others! Referrals are the heart of the real estate engine. Once clients have a good experience with you, they tell other people and create more business for you organically.

What's the most challenging part or stressful part of your job?

Making sure deadlines are met and juggling multiple tasks at one time. The biggest challenge is time away from family when meeting with clients on evenings and weekends, especially when my children were younger. You HAVE to have a supportive spouse as this is a demanding career.

What has been the most surprising thing about your job?

Doing something I love and being successful at it. Most days it doesn't feel like a job, and I have many clients that have become friends. Over my sixteen-year career I have won sales awards and recognition awards, but the most special was to be named 2020 Realtor of the Year by my fellow Realtors.

What kinds of qualities and personal attributes do you consider advantageous to doing your job successfully?

You have to be flexible as your schedule can change multiple times throughout the day. You have to be accommodating to your client's schedule. I try to match the personality of my client and get along with everyone.

How do you combat burnout?

Since I am doing something I love I honestly haven't gotten burnt out. Occasionally I need a break, but I can't wait to be back in action. You have to work when there is business to be had. In our local market the spring season is demanding, so I know I won't have a ton of personal time. As the season changes and the market slows down, I take that time to regroup, travel, and focus on my family and hobbies. My recommendation is to have a friend/teammate in real estate that you trust to back you up in your business for when you take a vacation or personal time.

How do you see your own career or the real estate field in general evolving in the future?

I have seen many changes in the last sixteen years in real estate. Some have made our jobs easier, and some have created more work. Most of the change has been technological with more Internet-based tools and services becoming available to Realtors and the general public. I have found that quickly adapting to change is the best approach as innovation won't wait for you to be comfortable. I plan to continue to evolve my services to meet the needs of my clients.

====

Summary

This chapter covered a lot of ground as far as looking more closely at the various types of jobs in real estate, how they differ, and what the pros and cons are of a career in this exciting field. Here are some ideas to take away with you as you move on to the next chapter:

- Real estate is an exciting and changing field that has historically had ups and downs and will likely continue to do so—yet it is a viable industry that is expected to see growth in the coming decade.
- No two days are alike for a real estate professional, which makes it an exciting field in which you are continuously challenged and constantly learning.
- As a real estate professional, you will have a nice mix of office hours (desk time) and time in the field, viewing properties, exploring areas, and meeting with clients or prospective clients.
- Real estate professionals can work with a variety of clients from all backgrounds, age groups, socioeconomic and geographic circumstances, and career and educational levels.

Given all you now know about the job of a real estate professional, you may still be questioning whether such a career is right for you. This chapter provided some questions that can help you visualize yourself in real-world situations you can expect to face on the job, to help you guide your decision process.

Assuming you are now more enthusiastic than ever about pursuing a career in real estate, in the next chapter we will look more closely at how you can refine your choice to a more specific job. It offers tips and advice on how to find the role and work environment that will be most satisfying to you, and what steps you can start taking—immediately!—toward reaching your future career goals.

2

Forming a Career Plan

Choosing a career may seem like one of the most difficult choices you will have to make, because it is one of the most important and there are so many options to consider. But it should not feel scary or daunting—it's actually a very exciting thing to think about. Often, it's easy to narrow down what type of careers suit your interests and personality, as you've seen in chapter 1. Other times, you can imagine yourself in many seemingly different careers, which is why it's important to think about what kinds of skills, characteristics, or interests are at the root of your career ambitions.

There are simply so many types of careers out there, and it is easy to feel overwhelmed. Particularly if you have many passions and interests, it can be hard to narrow your options down. Before you can plan the path to a successful career in the real estate field, it's important to think about what your expectations of the job are, and how you see it fitting in with other aspects of your life, such as where you want to live, how you want to balance life and work, and so on.

One benefit of pursuing real estate as a career is you have the flexibility to do it full- or part-time. Many people work in real estate while pursuing other interests, including other work or education. With real estate, as long as you keep required licenses up to date—and valid in the state in which you work— you can determine your own hours and even take breaks from real estate for a while if you choose.

This flexibility means you can work in real estate quite successfully and happily throughout your career, or you can do it for a period of time while deciding what you might want to do next, without putting yourself through years of post–high school education first. This is a positive thing regardless of your expectations of your work in real estate or how long term a career choice you think it will be for you.

While becoming a real estate agent or broker, or a property manager—the jobs we are mainly focusing on in this book—doesn't require much advanced education, these jobs don't themselves offer much room for long-term professional growth. The function of the job stays more or less the same, although technology and other external influences—such as the global pandemic that led to lockdowns and social distancing—might change some of the ways you actually perform tasks. This is great if it's what you love but something to consider if you think you may grow restless. It is possible to move to different types of jobs within the real estate realm—such as law, marketing, finance—but that requires an additional type of educational qualification.

All of this is to say, choosing a career path gives you a lot to think about, but fortunately it's also exciting to consider your options, particularly as it's a decision that is primarily based on aspects of you (your interests, natural gifts, curiosities) that you know more about than anyone else; and remember, people change career paths throughout their lives for all kinds of reasons. It's a serious decision, but it is not one you should fear is absolutely a final one.

Tip: This may all sound very overwhelming. Keep in mind as you consider your career options that it is common to change your mind or shift gears at any stage in your career. Be thoughtful about your decisions, but don't put too much pressure on yourself. It's not a case of only getting one chance to decide.

Also important to think about: How much education would you like to pursue? In most states, a high school diploma and a state license to work in real estate (which is usually valid for two years before you have to retest to renew— more on that later) is all that's required. However, you may have a desire to go to college for other reasons, or to earn a degree in an area that will further lend to your success in real estate, such as a degree in business or marketing.

A lot of choosing a career that "fits you" also comes down to personality and personal characteristics. Deciding on a career means asking yourself big questions, but there are several tools and assessment tests that can help you determine what your personal strengths and aptitudes are and with which career fields and environments they best align. These tools guide you to think about important factors in choosing a career path, such as how you respond to pressure and how effectively—and how much you enjoy—working and communicating with people. These will be discussed in this chapter as well.

Your Passions, Abilities, and Interests: In Job Form!

Think about how you've done at school and how things have worked out at any temporary or part-time jobs you've had so far. What are you really good at, in your opinion? And what have other people told you you're good at? What are you not very good at right now, but you would like to become better at? What are you not very good at, and you're okay with not getting better at?

Now forget about work for a minute. In fact, forget about needing to ever have a job again. You won the lottery—congratulations. Now answer these questions: What are your favorite three ways of spending your time? For each one of those things, can you describe why you think you in particular are attracted to it? If you could get up tomorrow and do anything you wanted all day long, what would it be? These questions can be fun but can also lead you to your true passions. The next step is to find the job that sparks your passions.

This chapter explores the educational requirements and other requirements for jobs in real estate, as well as options for where to go for help when planning your path to the career you want. It offers advice on how to begin preparing for your career path at any age or stage in your education, including in high school.

Planning the Plan

So where to begin? Before making the decision about how much post–high school education you want to pursue, if you haven't already earned a college degree, there are other considerations and steps you can take to map out your plan for pursuing your career. Preparing your career plan begins with developing a clear understanding of what your actual career goal is.

Planning your career path means asking yourself questions that will help shape a clearer picture of what your long-term career goals are and what steps to take to achieve them. When considering these questions, it's important to prioritize your answers—when listing your skills, for example, put them in order of strongest to weakest. When considering questions relating to how you want to balance your career with your nonwork life, such as family and hobbies, really think about what your top priorities are and in what order.

The following are questions that are helpful to think about deeply when planning your career path:

- Think about your interests outside of the work context. How do you like to spend your free time? What inspires you? What kind of people do you like to surround yourself with, and how do you best learn? What do you really love doing?
- Brainstorm a list of what appeals to you about working in real estate. Are you interested in helping people achieve their goals? Are you passionate about property or land development? Do you love meeting and working with new people? Do you like the idea of no day being the same? Are you attracted to a job that puts you in control of your time and lets you step away from a desk to work in the field? Work environment, schedule, the people you mix with daily: these are all important considerations.
- Research information on each job on your career choices list. You can find job descriptions, salary indications, career outlook, and educational requirements information online, for example. Some of this information was provided in chapter 1 of this book.
- Consider your personality traits. This is very important to finding which jobs "fit" you and which almost certainly do not. How do you respond to stress and pressure? Do you consider yourself a strong communicator? Do you work well in teams or prefer to work independently? Do you consider yourself a creative thinker? How do you respond to criticism? Are you curious and thorough? All of these are important to keep in mind to ensure you choose a career path that makes you happy and in which you can thrive.
- Although a career choice is obviously a huge factor in your future, it's important to consider what other factors feature in your vision of your ideal life. Think about how your career will fit in with the rest of your life, including whether you want to live in a big city or small town, how much flexibility you want in your schedule, how much autonomy you want in your work, and what your ultimate career goal is.

- Many job opportunities that offer experience to newcomers and recent graduates can come with relatively low salaries. In work like real estate, the less experience you have, the harder you will have to work to compete with seasoned professionals who have been at it way longer than you and have established reputations. What are your pay expectations, now and in the future?

Posing these questions to yourself and thinking about them deeply and answering them honestly will help make your career goals clearer and guide you in knowing which steps you will need to take to get there.

Visualize what you expect the work life of a real estate professional to be: which aspects appeal to you the most, which the least? As with any decision you make, consider carefully how well your career choice fits your personality and the other aspects of your life. *Ridofranz/iStock/Getty Images.*

WHERE TO GO FOR HELP

Again, the process of deciding on and planning a career path can be a little bit daunting. In many ways, the range of choices of careers available today is a wonderful thing. It allows us to refine our career goals and customize them to our own lives and personalities. In other ways, though, too much choice can be extremely confusing and requires a lot of soul-searching to navigate clearly.

Note: Depending on your age and educational level, you might also be thinking you have time to consider these points more carefully. But the sooner you start thinking in terms of a particular career path, the better prepared you will be to spot opportunities that present themselves in your schooling or your life to advance your relative skill sets.

REAL ESTATE AGENT OR REAL ESTATE BROKER? THE PROS AND CONS

It's not uncommon for a real estate agent to have the goal of becoming a broker eventually. Some people see it as a logical next step, while others really enjoy their work as an agent and have no desire to make the change.

Either is fine, but be sure you make an informed decision. If it's not clear what the actual difference is between a real estate agent and a broker, here's a quick explanation: To become a broker, you need to pass the broker license exam, in addition to the real estate license test required for both jobs. The main difference between a real estate agent and broker is that a real estate broker can own a firm or be an independent contractor, while a real estate agent must work under the supervision of a broker.

Here are some pros and cons of making the agent-to-broker leap, as explained by Kaplan Real Estate Education:[1]

1. **It may be the next logical step, but don't push yourself too fast.** Becoming a licensed broker is relatively easy assuming you already have a real estate license. Each state differs, but it's typical to need a minimum of two years of full-time licensed real estate salesperson experience (in the last five years) before taking the broker license exam. This means you could go for your broker license after just two years working as an agent. The downside to this is moving too fast. Your first couple of years on the job will already mean a period of adjustment and learning, and piling on an additional challenge of broker license exam preparation may be a lot too soon. So don't rush to what might seem like the next step.
2. **Real estate brokers have complete career autonomy—and a ton of responsibility.** As a broker, you can own your own real estate business. With hard work and strong business skills, you could grow this business to be well established in your community and to bring you great

success. You could step back from working directly with clients to focus on managing agents who work for you. It sounds fantastic, perhaps, and is very satisfying if it's the challenge you want and are prepared for. This autonomy that comes with being the boss comes with enormous responsibility for areas outside the client relationship, such as marketing, management, hiring and retaining agents, and ensuring that your business is run intelligently and legally. Not everyone wants the extra pressure of having increased responsibilities.

3. **Real estate brokers can earn more money—but with more overhead.** Being the boss means more opportunity to earn, which makes sense. As a broker, you earn a small percentage of your agents' commissions, in addition to any revenue you bring in from selling properties yourself. You get to keep your entire commission, of course, as you are working for yourself. If you're both managing agents who work for you and still selling properties yourself, you can make double or triple what you would as an agent working for another broker.

   There can be, however, a lot of overhead costs—money you need to invest up front—in order to launch your brokerage business. Office space rents can be high. You will need to invest in marketing. You may spend a lot of your extra earnings as a broker, at least initially, in bolstering your business. Having some savings set aside for the purpose of opening your own brokerage is essential to get your business off the ground.

4. **Brokers can work as little or as much as they want—but you need drive to succeed.** As your own boss, you can decide to work as little or as much as you want. This is a main theme when discussing the perks of a career in real estate, be it broker or agent. The amount of new responsibilities you take on is entirely up to you. You have lots of choices on how to run your business. You can be your only employee, or you can hire a team of agents to work for you. You can expand as much as you like, or keep things small. The amount of responsibility you take on, and indeed the amount of business, is up to you. However, it all hangs on your goals. As with anything, the more effort you put into your real estate broker career, the more it will grow and succeed. Sitting back and working when you feel like it will reflect in your business. Finding a balance in terms of time and energy spent on your business can be a challenge for new real estate brokers.

5. **Brokers can help real estate agents learn the industry.** Being a broker gives you an opportunity to give back to the industry by helping train new real estate agents who need guidance from the brokers and other agents they work with. As the more experienced real estate professional, and perhaps as the "boss" of these fresh employees, you have a chance to offer advice from your own experience and act as a mentor. This can be extremely fulfilling and also help benefit you by reminding you what makes a successful real estate professional. But it can also take up a lot of time and mental energy, so be prepared for that, so that your mentoring role does not become overly time consuming.

* * *

Answering questions about your habits, preferences, interests, and personality can be hard to do—and to do honestly. Identifying and prioritizing all your ambitions, interests, and passions is tough. It's not always easy to see ourselves objectively or see a way to achieve what matters most to us. But there are several resources and approaches to help guide you in drawing conclusions about these important questions.

- Take a career assessment test to help you answer questions about what career best suits you. There are several available online, which you can find via your search engine.
- Consult with a career or personal coach to help you refine your understanding of your goals and how to pursue them.
- Talk with professionals working in the job you are considering and ask them what they enjoy about their work, what they find the most challenging, and what path they followed to get there.
- Educate yourself as much as possible about the field: What are the latest business trends or technological advancements? Stay current as much as possible with topics relating to the career you wish to pursue.
- If possible, arrange to job shadow someone in the real estate field. To "job shadow" is to accompany someone during their workday to witness firsthand what a typical day on the job is like.

ONLINE RESOURCES TO HELP YOU PLAN YOUR PATH

The Internet is an excellent source of advice and assessment tools that can help you find and figure out how to pursue your career path. Some of these tools focus on an individual's personality and aptitude; others can help you identify and improve your skills to prepare for your career.

In addition to the sites below, you can use the Internet to find a career or life coach near you—many offer their services online as well. Job sites such as LinkedIn are a good place to search for people working in a profession you'd like to learn more about or to explore the types of jobs available in real estate.

- At educations.com, you will find a career test designed to help you find the job of your dreams. Visit https://www.educations.com/career-test to take the test.
- The Princeton Review has created a career quiz that focuses on personal interests: https://www.princetonreview.com/quiz/career-quiz.
- The Bureau of Labor Statistics provides information, including quizzes and videos, to help students up to grade twelve explore various career paths. The site also provides general information on career prospects and salaries. Visit BLS.gov to find these resources.

Note: Young adults with disabilities can face additional challenges when planning a career path. DO-IT (Disabilities, Opportunities, Internetworking, and Technology) is an organization dedicated to promoting career and education inclusion for everyone. Its website contains a wealth of information and tools to help all young people plan a career path, including self-assessment tests and career exploration questionnaires: https://www.washington.edu/doit/preparing-career-online-tutorial.

Making High School Count

Once you have narrowed down your interests and have a fairly solid idea what type of career you want to pursue, you naturally want to start putting your career path plan into motion as quickly as you can. If you are a high school student, you may feel there isn't much you can do toward achieving your career goals—other than, of course, earning good grades and graduating.

But there are actually many ways you can make your high school years count toward your career in the real estate industry before you have earned your high school diploma. This section will cover how you can use this period of your education and life to better prepare you for your career goal and to ensure you keep your passion alive while improving your skill set.

Even while still in high school, there are many ways you can begin working toward your career goal. Classes in another language, in math, in interpersonal communication, and in business can all help you prepare for a career in the real estate industry. *monkeybusinessimages/iStock/Getty Images.*

COURSES TO TAKE IN HIGH SCHOOL

Depending on your high school and what courses are offered and that you have access to, there are many subjects that will help you prepare for a career in real estate. Beyond doing your own research into different aspects of the real estate job you really like and the type of work you see yourself enjoying in the future, you can take advantage of courses, particularly any college prep courses, that your school offers that will help you with your career goals. For real estate, take classes particularly in areas relating to business or economics, but also in subjects such as public speaking or even literature to help you strengthen your communication skills.

Tip: Everybody harbors biases in the way they think about sensitive issues such as race and sexual identity. To find out whether you have biases of which you may be unaware, check out this test online, which was developed at Harvard University: https://implicit.harvard.edu/implicit/takeatest.html.

Here are some courses, college prep or standard level, that you should pursue while in high school. Some of them may seem unrelated initially, but they will all help you prepare yourself and develop key skills.

Math. Dealing with square footage of homes, costs of properties, managing your own commission-based income—all of this will require savvy math skills.

Interpersonal communication and public speaking. These courses will be an asset in any profession, but especially in the real estate industry. So much of your job will potentially be interacting with colleagues in teams or directly with clients. You need to communicate clearly and effectively; you also need to be able to connect with clients so that they trust you and know they can rely on you.

A second language. You will work with clients from all cultural backgrounds, and being able to communicate in more than one language may not only give you an edge in gaining new business, but it can make the entire experience more comfortable and informed for everyone involved.

Business and economics. As an entrepreneur, you need to have some business basics. And you might find yourself operating your own brokerage, which will demand even more business and economics know-how. You will also want to deeply understand patterns in the real estate business that you read about in the news. Classes in business and economics will help you understand how to run or work in any business, including in the real estate industry.

Tip: Taking advanced placement (AP) courses while in high school (assuming you pass the AP exam at the end of the course) may enable you to earn college credit early and skip taking elementary or introductory courses in the subject (for example, business) if and when you get to college.

HOW REAL ESTATE PROFESSIONALS PRACTICE SELF-CARE

"Self-care" refers to the various ways people can ensure that they are looking after their own needs: eating and sleeping well, for example, or taking exercise to release energy and process thoughts in a healthy, beneficial way. Doing so can help anyone—especially people in high-stress careers—maintain their own sense of well-being so they are better prepared and able to help others and avoid burnout. The following tips for how to practice self-care are provided by licensed social worker Jane E. Shersher:[2]

1. **Focus on your breathing.** Take long, slow, deep breaths as a way of maintaining your calm and relaxing your mind. Consider setting a timer to remind yourself to breathe in this way a few times a day for a minute or two at a time. It may sound a little strange to remind yourself to breathe, but doing so in this manner can lead to noticeable results.

2. **Do a body scan.** This might also sound a bit odd, but you can help your body and mind relax by paying attention to each body part one at a time from head to toe, concentrating on it and checking for points of tension to release.

3. **Guided imagery.** Visualize yourself in a place or an environment that helps to calm you down, inspire you, or aid you in focusing for stretches of time (a few minutes, for example). There are apps you can use to listen to soothing sounds, such as nature sounds, to help you feel calm.

4. **Practice mindfulness.** Mindfulness has certainly gained in popularity over the last several years. It is the practice of focusing your awareness on the present moment, while noticing and accepting feelings, thoughts, and bodily sensations. There are several apps that offer guided mindfulness meditations that you can try.

5. **Practice yoga, tai chi, or qigong.** These are physical exercises for the body and mind that help with mental focus, flexibility, and balance and can reduce anxiety. You can incorporate these several times a day.

6. **Get enough sleep.** Sleep is so important that it cannot be stressed enough. Your body should be getting, on average, seven to eight hours of sleep every night. Try to build a routine that helps you be able to fall into a sleepy state so you can have a restful night. Exercise, diet, and winding-down routines (like taking a bath, reading a book) can help.

Educational Requirements

As mentioned earlier, there is no post–high school degree requirement for launching your career in real estate. A high school diploma or equivalent is all you need to take your state's real estate agent license test, and later the broker test if you desire. Licensure—which needs to be renewed usually every two years or anytime you want to work in real estate in another state—is the only requirement post–high school that you will need to start working in real estate. However, you may decide to earn a degree anyway, for personal or professional reasons. Having a degree will only be an asset to you, whatever your career goals.

"I have seen many changes in the last sixteen years in real estate. Some have made our jobs easier, and some have created more work. Most of the change has been technological with more Internet-based tools and services becoming available to Realtors and the general public. I have found that quickly adapting to change is the best approach as innovation won't wait for you to be comfortable. I plan to continue to evolve my services to meet the needs of my clients."—Laura Soride, Realtor

WHY CHOOSE AN ASSOCIATE'S DEGREE?

This degree takes comparably shorter time and coursework to complete, as related to other advanced degrees you might consider, and if you are living near a community college, that adds a layer of convenience.

A two-year degree—called an associate's degree—is sufficient to give you a knowledge base to begin your career and can form as a basis should you decide to pursue a four-year degree later. Do keep in mind, though, that jobs in real estate can be quite competitive. If you are prepared to put in the financial and time commitment to earn an associate's degree and are sure of the career goal you have set for yourself, consider earning a bachelor's instead. With so much competition out there, the more chance to stand out you can give yourself, the greater your successes will be.

HOW TO BECOME A PROPERTY MANAGER

We've talked a lot about real estate agents and brokers, but what about property managers? If this is your goal, you will follow most of the same steps as with the other real estate professions—including, in many cases, earning your real estate license. But the jobs are quite different. As a property manager, you will be largely responsible for important tasks like setting the rental rate for the property and collecting rent from tenants. You'll likely be the one advertising rental properties and drawing potential tenants, whose application you'll review (as well as screening the tenants themselves). You'll show the property and then manage it, taking care of its maintenance. It's a lot of responsibility. So how do you land a job as a property manager? Here are five steps as outlined by Mashvisor.com:[3]

1. **Understand the legal requirements for the job.** Each state has its own requirements for becoming a property manager, and it's important to know the laws in your state. You can read more about this at All PropertyManagement.com.[4] States also usually have certain requirements relating to age, real estate education, experience, and residency, and some require you to pass an exam.

2. **Earn your required real estate education.** This again will vary by state. While it may not be a strict requirement, the reality is, to secure a good job in this field, it's increasingly expected that you have taken some courses in real estate development, management, finance, urban planning, and affordable housing administration. And many companies seek candidates with real estate training or a license.

3. **Obtain specialized certifications.** There are quite a few available to potential property managers:

   - *National apartment leasing professional (NALP) certification.* This teaches new property managers the skills to become more proficient and effective at their jobs.
   - *Certified apartment manager (CAM) certification.* This is targeted at on-site managers who are often the only property managers whom apartment residents will deal with on a daily basis.

- *Certified property manager (CPM) certification.* This is usually attained to distinguish you from competitors while being a helpful certification for starting a property management company.
- *Master property manager (MPM) certification.* This is the highest distinction a residential property manager can attain. With this certification, you'll be recognized as a leader in the industry and a versatile residential property professional.

4. **Find properties to manage!** This obviously is easier said than done, but it's very possible with the right attitude and energy. As with any job search, networking is key. Talk to people in your area about your career goals and learn about any opportunities that way. Search online for job leads. Be persistent, and stay updated on best practices.

5. **Stay up to date in your field.** Even after you've been working for a while, in any field it's a good idea to ensure you are not slipping in your performance by keeping up to date on best or changing practices, making sure certifications are up to date, and looking for professional development opportunities like night or online classes.

WHY CHOOSE A BACHELOR'S DEGREE?

A bachelor's degree—which usually takes four years to obtain—is not a requirement for many real estate careers. But in general, the higher education you pursue, the better your odds are to advance in your career, which means more opportunity and often more compensation.

The difference between an associate's and a bachelor's degree is of course the amount of time each takes to complete. To earn a bachelor's degree, a candidate must complete forty college credits, compared with twenty for an associate's. This translates to more courses completed and a deeper exploration of degree content, even though similar content is covered in both.

Note: Even when not required, continuing your education as far as possible can help advance your career, give you an edge over the competition in the field, and give you more specific knowledge relating to your work in the real estate industry.

WHY CHOOSE A MASTER'S DEGREE?

A master's degree is an advanced degree that usually takes two years to complete. A master's will offer you a chance to become more specialized and to build on the education and knowledge you gained while earning your bachelor's. A master's can be done directly after your bachelor's, although many people choose to work for a while in between to discover what type of master's degree is most relevant to their careers and interests. Many people also earn their master's degree while working full- or part-time.

Note: Although a high school diploma or equivalent was once all that was required to become a property manager, the number of property management companies who prefer to hire college graduates is increasing. Many property managers also have real estate licenses, but in addition to that, increasingly they are pursuing bachelor's or master's degrees in real estate, business administration, public administration, finance, or accounting. It's something to consider to give yourself that extra edge.

HELPING OTHERS ACCOMPLISH THEIR GOALS

Born and raised in New Jersey, Janis DeVito has been a Morristown, New Jersey, resident for more than twenty-five years. Janis began her career as a software developer before obtaining her master's degree in management. She enjoyed working in dot-com and technology consulting businesses before finally making the switch into the residential real estate world in 2001. "I worked on Wall Street during 9/11. I was lucky that I missed my train that day; I then decided I needed to get out of the city. I had always had an interest in real estate as I had sold two of my own houses. I obtained my real estate license and was hired by one of the larger companies as a manager apprentice. I spent twelve years with that organization before branching out on my own."

With a strong background in training, recruiting, organizing, managing, and real estate acumen, Janis created West End Residential (WE Residential) and is the owner and broker of record. An avid sports lover, she enjoys attending sporting events as well as spending time with her daughter and their two dogs, Molly and Maisie. Janis's special skills include a wonderfully infectious laugh and awesome dance moves.

* * *

How did you choose real estate as a career?

I've always enjoyed people, and sales was natural because I like to help people accomplish things.

Can you describe your educational background and career path to date?

I have a bachelor of science degree in computer science from East Stroudsburg University and a master of science in management from Stevens Institute of Technology.

What is a typical day on the job for you?

No two days are the same. I spend my days working on marketing for the business (I own the company), recruiting, coaching/training the agents, working on the "back office" for the business, handling "got a minute?" [moments] to help agents solve problems, and still listing and selling on occasion. I have been leading people in residential real estate for a long time, so my experience comes in handy every day (twenty years).

What's the best or most satisfying part of your job?

When my coaching helps an agent find success.

What's the most challenging part or stressful part of your job?

Not necessarily challenging, but very important to keep my company and my agents in front of the competition by staying educated, empowered, and armed with the latest tools and technology.

What has been the most surprising thing about your job?

By meeting so many people, both agents and consumers, you get to learn all types of perspectives and cultures. You hone your communication skills as a result. This, in turn, makes you calm when you are dealing with all aspects of your life, professional and personal.

What kinds of qualities and personal attributes do you consider advantageous to doing your job successfully?

You have to like ALL types of people. You must be organized. You must be trustworthy. As a business, WE succeed by being free from a centralized decision-making corporate structure, [allowing] our brokerage the ability to respond as needed to everything from local micro market shifts to press inquiries. When you are able to adjust branding, marketing, and processes without approval from a corporate entity, you add vitality and timeliness to everything you do. WE are striving to be nimble, and this has given us a responsive company culture. WE can perceive small shifts in operations and effectiveness, and WE adjust accordingly. This helps our agents and our buyers and sellers have an automatic leg up in their real estate transactions.

How do you combat burnout?

I take breaks every month and make sure that I have someone who can help cover me if I am unavailable. Communicating my "break" helps my agents and customers understand and not get worried that they are not being helped.

How do you see your own career or the real estate field in general evolving in the future?

The growth of West End Residential has been and continues to be completely organic. Our focus on intentional hiring allowed us to hire thirteen agents in 2019, bringing our agent total to just under forty agents. I see opening other offices and providing other service offerings over time. Our dedication to relevant, customized, and ongoing training has enabled 78 percent of our agents to close deals in 2019. Additionally, WE created our Legacy Agent Program and hired our first legacy agent who has over fifty years of experience in the real estate business!

Summary

This chapter covered a lot of ground in terms of how to break down the challenge of not only discovering whether a career in the real estate industry is right for you and in what environment, capacity, and work culture you want to work, but also how best to prepare yourself for achieving your career goal.

In this chapter, you learned about some of the specific training and educational options, requirements, and expectations that will put you, no matter what your current education level or age, at a strong advantage in a competitive field. Use this chapter as a guideline for how to best discover what type of career will be the right fit for you and consider what steps you can already be taking to get there. Some tips to leave you with:

- Take time to carefully consider what kind of work environment you see yourself working in, and what kind of schedule, interaction with colleagues, work culture, and responsibilities you want to have.
- Pay attention to current research and issues relating to the field of real estate and in particular to the area of the field in which you want to work.
- Talk with a professional to get a feeling for what hours they keep, what challenges they face, and what the overall job entails. Find out what education or training they completed before launching their career.
- Investigate various colleges and certification options so you can better prepare yourself for the next step in your career path. (More of this in chapter 3.)
- Don't feel you have to wait until you graduate from high school to begin taking steps to accomplish your career goals.
- Keep work/life balance in mind. The career you choose will be one of many adult decisions you make, and ensuring that you keep all your priorities—family, location, work schedule—in mind will help you choose the right career for you, which will make you a happier person.

3

Pursuing the Educational Path

*M*aking decisions about your educational path can be just as complex a process as choosing a career in the first place. It is a decision that not only demands understanding what kind of education or training is required for the career you want, but also what kind of school or college you want to attend and, of course, how you are going to pay for it. Everyone has different circumstances that need to be taken into consideration, be they geographical or economical. There is a lot to consider no matter what area of study you want to pursue and depending on the type of job you want to have within the field of real estate.

Now that you've gotten an overview of the different degree options that can prepare you for your future career as a real estate professional, this chapter will dig more deeply into how to best choose the right type of study plan for you. Even if you are years away from earning your high school diploma or equivalent, it's never too soon to start weighing your options, thinking about the application process, and of course taking time to really consider what kind of educational track and environment will suit you best.

Not everyone wants to take time to go to college or pursue additional academic-based training, and for many careers it is not required, even if recommended. However, depending on what kind of career you want to pursue in the real estate arena, some level of higher education will most likely be required. Job training, at minimum, will be required no matter what field you work in, and in some cases earning a university degree will be mandatory.

So if you are interested in and prepared to follow the post–high school (or advanced) educational path, this chapter will help you navigate the process of deciding on the type of institution you would most thrive in, determining what type of degree you want to earn, and looking into costs and how to find help in meeting them.

The chapter will also give you advice on the application process, how to prepare for any entrance exams such as the SAT or ACT that you may need to take, and how to communicate your passion, ambition, and personal experience in a personal statement. When you've completed this chapter, you should have a good sense of what kind of post–high school education is right for you and how to ensure you have the best chance of being accepted at the institution of your choice.

> **Note:** At the time of writing, the US and beyond are coming out of a pandemic that has caused some of the traditional approaches to teaching and learning to change—hopefully just temporarily. This chapter is offering advice that assumes you will be applying to and attending educational institutions in person, which will hopefully be the case. Even if, for now, you are learning or doing "campus visits" virtually, the advice offered here is still relevant, even if the way you engage with institutions, faculty members, or other students is a bit unorthodox for the time being.

Finding a Program or School That Fits Your Personality

Before we get into the details of good schools that offer degrees in subjects related to careers in the real estate industry, it's a good idea for you to take some time to consider what "type" of school will be best for you. Just as with your future work environment, understanding how you best learn, what type of atmosphere best fits your personality, and how and where you are most likely to succeed will play a major part in how happy you will be with your choice. This section will provide some thinking points to help you refine what kind of school or program is the best fit for you.

CONSIDERING A GAP YEAR

Taking a year off between high school and college, often called a gap year, is normal, perfectly acceptable, and even increasingly seen as a strong enhancement to a college application. Particularly if you want to pursue a career in real estate, no matter in what capacity, having exposure to the world outside of the classroom will help you gain perspective and experience that you can immediately apply to your future work. It can help you become more empathetic, less judgmental, and a more open thinker. Because the cost of college has gone up dramatically, it literally pays for you to know going in what you want to study, and a gap year—well spent—can do lots to help you answer that question. It can also give you an opportunity to explore different places and people to help you find a deeper sense of what you'd like to study when your gap year has ended.

Some great ways to spend your gap year include joining the Peace Corps or another organization that offers opportunities for work experience. A gap year can help you see things from a new perspective. Consider enrolling in a mountaineering program or other gap year–styled program, backpacking across Europe or other countries on the cheap (be safe and bring a friend), finding a volunteer organization that furthers a cause you believe in or that complements your career aspirations, joining a Road Scholar program (see www.roadscholar.org), teaching English in another country (see https://www.gooverseas.com/blog/best-countries-for-seniors -to-teach-english-abroad for more information), or working and earning money for college.

Many students will find that they get much more out of college when they have a year to mature and to experience the real world. The American Gap Year Association reports from its alumni surveys that students who take gap years show improved civic engagement, improved college graduation rates, and improved GPAs in college. Check out https://gapyearassociation.org/ for lots of advice and resources if you're considering a potentially life-altering experience.

If nothing else, answering questions like the following ones can help you narrow your search and focus on a smaller sampling of choices. Write down your answers to these questions somewhere where you can refer to them often, such as in your notes app on your phone:

Size. Does the size of the school matter to you? Colleges and universities range from sizes of five hundred or fewer students to twenty-five thousand students. If you are considering college or university, think about what size class you would like, and what the right instructor-to-student ratio is for you.

Community location. Would you prefer to be in a rural area, a small town, a suburban area, or a large city? How important is the location of the school in the larger world to you? Is the flexibility of an online degree or certification program attractive to you, or do you prefer more on-site, hands-on instruction?

Length of study. How many months or years do you want to put into your education before you start working professionally?

Housing options. If applicable, what kind of housing would you prefer? Dorms, off-campus apartments, and private homes are all common options.

Student body. How would you like the student body to "look"? Think about coed versus all-male and all-female settings, as well as the makeup of minorities, how many students are part-time versus full-time, and the percentage of commuter students.

Academic environment. Consider which majors are offered and at which levels of degree. Research the student-to-faculty ratio. Are the classes taught often by actual professors or more often by the teaching assistants? Find out how many internships the school typically provides to students. Are independent study or study abroad programs available in your area of interest?

Financial aid availability/cost. Does the school provide ample opportunities for scholarships, grants, work-study programs, and the like? Does cost play a role in your options? (For most people, it does.)

Support services. Investigate the strength of the academic and career placement counseling services of the school.

Social activities and athletics. Does the school offer clubs that you are interested in? Which sports are offered? Are scholarships available?

Specialized programs. Does the school offer honors programs or programs for veterans or students with disabilities or special needs?

Note: Not all these questions are going to be important to you, and that's fine. Be sure to make note of aspects that don't matter so much to you too, such as size or location. You might change your mind as you go to visit colleges, but it's important to make note of where you are to begin with.

U.S. News & World Report puts it best when it says the college that fits you best is one that will do all these things:[1]

- Offer a degree that matches your interests and needs.
- Provide a style of instruction that matches the way you like to learn.
- Provide a level of academic rigor to match your aptitude and preparation.
- Offer a community that feels like home to you.
- Value you for what you do well.

MAKE THE MOST OF CAMPUS VISITS

If it's at all practical and feasible, you should visit the campuses of all the schools you're considering. To get a real feel for any college or university, you need to walk around the campus, spend some time in the common areas where students hang out, and sit in on a few classes. You can also sign up for campus tours, which are typically given by current students. This is another good way to see the campus and ask questions of someone who knows. Be sure to visit the specific school/building that covers your possible major as well. The website and brochures won't be able to convey that intangible feeling you'll get from a visit.

In addition to the questions listed in the earlier section in this chapter titled "Finding a Program or School That Fits Your Personality," consider these questions as well. Make a list of questions that are important to you before you visit.

- What is the makeup of the current freshman class? Is the campus diverse?
- What is the meal plan like? What are the food options?
- Where do most of the students hang out between classes? (Be sure to visit this area.)
- How long does it take to walk from one end of the campus to the other?
- What types of transportation are available for students? Does campus security provide escorts to cars, dorms, and so forth at night?

To be ready for your visit and make the most of it, consider these tips and words of advice. Before you go:

- Be sure to do some research. At the least, spend some time on the college website. Make sure your questions aren't addressed adequately there first.
- Make a list of questions.
- Arrange to meet with a professor in your area of interest or to visit the specific school.
- Be prepared to answer questions about yourself and why you are interested in this school.
- Dress in neat, clean, and casual clothes. Avoid wrinkled clothing or anything with stains.
- Listen and take notes.
- Don't interrupt.
- Be positive and energetic.
- Make eye contact when someone speaks directly to you.
- Ask questions.
- Thank people for their time.

Finally, be sure to send thank-you notes or emails after the visit is over. Remind the recipient when you visited the campus and thank them for their time.

* * *

The aim of this section has been to impress upon you the importance of finding the right fit for your chosen learning institution. Take some time to paint a mental picture about the kind of university or school setting that will best complement your needs. Then read on for specifics about each degree.

> **Note:** In the academic world, accreditation matters, and it is something you should consider when choosing a school. Accreditation is basically a seal of approval that schools promote to let prospective students feel sure the institution will provide a quality education that is worth the investment and will help graduates reach their career goals. Future employers will want to see that the program you completed has such a seal of quality, so it's something to keep in mind when choosing a school.

Determining Your Education Plan

There are many options, as mentioned, when it comes to pursuing an education in the real estate field. These include two-year community colleges and four-year colleges, and master's programs and PhD programs. This section will focus on undergraduate, or bachelor's, programs that can help you prepare for your career.

HOW TO HAVE A GAP YEAR DURING (OR JUST FOLLOWING) A PANDEMIC

Although an earlier section in this chapter explored options for spending a gap year that would certainly offer invaluable experience, unfortunately currently they are not all viable options due to the coronavirus—but that does not mean there aren't enriching activities and pursuits you can engage in to make a gap year just as worthwhile.

NextAdvisor offers some tips on how to make the most of a gap year,[2] even if it is not possible to participate in a structured program such as the Peace Corps. While these tips may not seem as exciting as traveling abroad, the point of a gap year is to help you refine your interests and gain additional skills before committing yourself to a college program. Here are some options to consider:

- Learn a new skill. Learn a new language. Become an expert in building an online platform if you want to grow your own private practice or reach a broader audience in the future online. Take a photography course. It's a good time to really develop yourself in new areas that may directly or indirectly affect you in your future career, in that it can help you to look at the world and people differently.
- Read. Science has shown that reading fiction makes us more empathetic,[3] which is a key skill for anyone to improve.
- Get a job to save money for college. The coronavirus has also hit many hard financially, so taking a year to earn money before heading off to school is certainly a valuable use of your time.
- Volunteer. There are virtual volunteer programs (check out VolunteerMatch. org) or you can do more local volunteering, such as buying groceries for an elderly neighbor.

- Seek out remote internships. Many people are currently working at home, and there are opportunities for interns to do the same.
- Take online classes. You can enroll at a local community college in a related subject. Whether you are opting for a two-year or four-year degree—and possibly later a master's or even a PhD—you will find there are many choices. It's a good idea to select roughly five to ten schools in a realistic location (for you) that offer the degree you want to earn. If you are considering online programs, include these in your list.

Tip: Consider attending a university in your resident state (where you live and pay taxes), if possible, which will save you lots of money if you attend a state school. Private institutions don't typically discount resident student tuition costs.

Be sure you research the basic GPA and SAT or ACT requirements of each school as well. Although some community colleges do not require standardized tests for the application process, others do.

Note: If you are planning to apply to a college or program that requires the ACT or SAT, advisors recommend that students take both the ACT and the SAT during their junior year of high school (spring at the latest). You can retake these tests and use your highest score, so be sure to leave time to retake early senior year if needed. You want your best scores to be available to all the schools you're applying to by January of your senior year, which will also enable them to be considered with any scholarship applications. Keep in mind these are general timelines—be sure to check the exact deadlines and calendars of the schools to which you're applying.

THE SAT IS OPTIONAL—SHOULD I TAKE IT ANYWAY?

One of the consequences of the coronavirus pandemic as it relates to education is that many universities changed aspects of their application processes. More than half of four-year colleges and universities in the US—a staggering percentage—decided to make entrance exams like the SAT and ACT optional in 2021,[4] and this is a change that may sustain for a lot longer.

What exactly does "test optional" mean? It varies from school to school. Be sure you know what it means for any school you are considering applying to:

- Truly test optional means you decide if you want to submit your test scores. If you do, the scores will be taken into consideration along with other parts of the application. This implies that the test scores may carry less weight when compared with the other application elements but will be considered.
- "Test-flexible" schools will allow you to submit scores for the SAT or ACT, or a different test in their place (such as a SAT Subject Test or AP test).
- "Test-blind" schools will not consider any scores, even if you include them in the application. If you feel confident that your scores will be an asset to your application, then by all means take the test and submit the score. It will not hurt your chances and can only help them. And if you take the test and are not satisfied that the results will give your application a positive edge, then you are not obligated to submit the scores. So you really can't lose by preparing for and taking the tests.

Once you have found five to ten schools in a realistic location for you that offer the degree you want, spend some time on their websites studying the requirements for admissions. Important factors weighing on your decision of what schools to apply to should include whether you meet the requirements, your chances of getting in (but aim high!), tuition costs and availability of scholarships and grants, location, and the school's reputation and licensure/graduation rates.

Note: Most colleges and universities will list the average stats for the last class accepted to the program, which will give you a sense of your chances of acceptance.

The order of these characteristics will depend on your grades and test scores, your financial resources, your work experience, and other personal factors. Taking everything into account, you should be able to narrow your list down to the institutions or schools that best match your educational or professional goals as well as your resources and other factors such as location and duration of study.

CHOOSING AN EDUCATIONAL PATH FOR YOUR SPECIFIC CAREER GOAL

Depending on your career goals, you may want to pursue varying levels of post–high school education to prepare for or grow in your career. You do not need a college degree to become a real estate agent or broker or to become a property manager. However, if it is your goal to run your own successful business, then taking business courses, if not earning a full college degree, is something you should consider deeply.

When considering what education to pursue after high school, it's good to keep some ideas in mind. For one, some schools and programs have stronger reputations than others. Although you can certainly have a successful and satisfying career and experience without going to the "number one" school in your field of study, it is a good idea to shop around, to compare different schools and get a sense of what they offer and what features of each are the most important—or least important—to you.

Keep in mind that what is "great" for one person may not be as great for someone else. What might be a perfect school for you might be too difficult, too expensive, or not rigorous enough for someone else. Keep in mind the advice of the previous sections when deciding what you really need in a school.

Consider your options in terms of what you expect to or desire to achieve as an end goal, in the context not only of your career goals but what career goals you may develop as you move forward in your career. For example, you may not need a bachelor's degree to get an entry-level job in your field of choice, but down the road, as your aspirations and experience develop, you may find having one would be a strong asset if not a set requirement.

Educational Requirements for Real Estate Careers

As mentioned previously, there are no hard-and-fast educational requirements for a career as a real estate agent or broker or a property manager other than a high school degree or equivalent and the necessary license to work in your state. However, this does not mean you shouldn't consider pursuing higher education after high school, if you haven't already, whether it be before you begin working or part-time while you are already working in real estate.

NON–REAL ESTATE DEGREES TO CONSIDER

Business administration. Anyone considering starting and operating their own business will logically gain from having a background in business administration, a degree that focuses on learning to be an effective and influential business leader.

Graphic design. Graphic design, like marketing or photography degree programs, will help you promote and advertise your business and yourself. Being able to create your own ads and other visuals and publications will save you loads of money from hiring others to create your promotional materials for you.

Digital marketing. For a self-employed person, promotion is absolutely essential to your survival and success in business. Digital marketing enables you to promote yourself and your services to attract clients, as well as advertise properties to get them rented or sold as quickly as possible.

Accounting. An accounting degree will teach you how to review and manage ledgers, as well as do things like process debit and credit card transactions in addition to other payment methods. This is all relevant to a real estate professional.

Human resources. If you are running your own business, you will be responsible for recruiting and managing staff. Building and managing a team requires skills in managing conflict, navigating potential legal territory, and other potentially sticky challenges that a background in human resources will help you navigate.

Finance. This area of study will arm you with important economic understanding so you will know how to manage your own finances as well as make educated predictions in trends and markets to know where you would be wise to invest.

Psychology. Studying psychology, you will learn the basics of human behavior and why people do the things they do. This is key to any sales profession. A psychology program teaches you about emotions and how people manage them and can give you valuable insights into human behavior.

Entrepreneurship. Real estate professionals are at their core entrepreneurs. Entrepreneurship degree plans cover law, marketing, business, accounting, and other subjects relevant to preparing you to launch and run a successful entrepreneurial venture.

Photography. Photography is a major aspect of real estate sales, used in advertising properties and drawing viewers. Photography classes show you how to use lighting and perspective and other tools and approaches to capture a property at its absolute best.

Computer science. While this may seem an unrelated if not unlikely choice of study for a future real estate profession, the reality is real estate agents spend an awful lot of time on their computers, and if you are running your own business you will benefit from being your own IT department, with the ability to set up and manage printers and other devices required to run a real estate business, and to set up and maintain local area networks and wide area networks.

In this section, we look at the post–high school education or training options to consider for the jobs in real estate. I'll point you to schools that focus on real estate education, as well as other areas of study that are relevant to a career in real estate and that can provide you with a relevant set of skills to apply to your future role in real estate.

Note: Although not everyone needs or wants to spend the time and money on a college degree, it is worth taking the time to consider the option. If your priority is to start working and earning as soon as possible, it's understandable that pursuing more education first might seem undesirable. But long term, it may open up more career options or provide you with a stronger foundation of knowledge in your career.

A college degree in real estate is the most obvious college track to pursue if you are set on a future in real estate. Programs in real estate and property management degrees or certificate programs teach students skills and approaches to overseeing residential, commercial, or industrial real estate on behalf of owners.

Real estate degree or certificate programs teach students important skills such as managing budgets, advertising rental places, and selling. Classes focus on finance, negotiation, managing reports, property laws, life safety, and environmental issues.

According to *U.S. News & World Report*, here are the top ten schools offering real estate programs in the US:[5]

University of Pennsylvania, based in Philadelphia, Pennsylvania
University of Wisconsin, Madison, based in Madison, Wisconsin
University of California, Berkeley, based in Berkeley, California
New York University, based in New York, New York
University of Texas at Austin, based in Austin, Texas
University of Florida, based in Gainesville, Florida
University of Southern California, based in Los Angeles, California
Florida State University, based in Tallahassee, Florida
University of Georgia, based in Athens, Georgia
University of North Carolina, Chapel Hill, based in Chapel Hill, North Carolina

WRITING A GREAT PERSONAL STATEMENT FOR ADMISSION

The personal statement you include with your application to college is extremely important, especially when your GPA and SAT/ACT scores are on the border of what is typically accepted. Write something that is thoughtful and conveys your understanding of the profession you are interested in, as well as your desire to practice in this field. Why are you uniquely qualified? Why are you a good fit for this university? These essays should be highly personal (the "personal" in personal statement). Will the admissions professionals who read it, along with hundreds of others, come away with a snapshot of who you really are and what you are passionate about?

Look online for some examples of good ones, which will give you a feel for what works. Be sure to check your specific school for length guidelines, format requirements, and any other guidelines they expect you to follow.

And of course, be sure to proofread it several times and ask a professional (such as your school writing center or your local library services) to proofread it as well.

What's It Going to Cost You?

So, the bottom line—what will your education end up costing you? First, some good news: According to *U.S. News & World Report*, the average tuition costs for colleges fell in 2020, which went against the standard trend of cost going up each year. For private colleges, costs fell by about 5 percent; for in-state colleges, the costs fell by 4 percent, and that of out-of-state (tuition for a person attending a state school but not in their resident state) has fallen by 6 percent.[6]

Note: According to *U.S. News & World Report*, the cost of an out-of-state school compared with an in-state school is 72 percent higher,[7] so looking for a school in the state in which you are a resident is definitely a way to cut down the costs of your education.

This trend appears to be continuing, according to an update by *U.S. News & World Report* that looks at tuition rates for the 2021–2022 school year.[8] This comes amid some calls for a tuition discount, as the COVID-19 pandemic has forced so many institutions to move to online course delivery.

In addition, there are several financial aid options to help you find the funding to earn the degree you want. We cover those next.

School can be an expensive investment, but there are many ways to seek help paying for your education. *marchmeena29/iStock/Getty Images.*

Financial Aid: Finding Money for Education

Finding the money to attend college can seem out of reach. But you can do it if you have a plan before you actually start applying to college. If you get into your top-choice university, don't let the sticker cost turn you away. Financial aid can come from many different sources, and it's available to cover all different kinds of costs you'll encounter during your years in college, including tuition, fees, books, housing, and food.

The good news is that universities more often offer incentive or tuition discount aid to encourage students to attend. The market is often more competitive in the favor of the student, and colleges and universities are responding by offering more generous aid packages to a wider range of students than they used to. Here are some basic tips and pointers about the financial aid process:

- You apply for financial aid during your senior year. You must fill out the FAFSA (Free Application for Federal Student Aid) form at studentaid. gov, which can be filed starting October 1 of your senior year until June of the year you graduate. Because the amount of available aid is limited, it's best to apply as soon as you possibly can.
- Be sure to compare and contrast deals you get at different schools. There is room to negotiate with universities. The first offer for aid may not be the best you'll get.
- Wait until you receive all offers from your top schools, and then use this information to negotiate with your top choice to see if it will match or beat the best aid package you received.
- To be eligible to keep and maintain your financial aid package, you must meet certain grade/GPA requirements. Be sure you are very clear on these academic expectations and keep up with them.
- You must reapply for federal aid every year.

Note: Watch out for scholarship scams! You should never be asked to pay to submit the FAFSA form ("free" is in its name) or be required to pay a lot to find appropriate aid and scholarships. These are free services. If an organization promises you you'll get aid or that you have to "act now or miss out," these are both warning signs of a less reputable organization. Also, be careful with your personal information to avoid identity theft as well. Simple things like closing and exiting your browser after visiting sites where you entered personal information goes a long way. Don't share your student aid ID number with anyone either.

It's important to understand the different forms of financial aid that are available to you. That way, you'll know how to apply for different kinds and get the best financial aid package that fits your needs and strengths. The two main categories that financial aid falls under are gift aid, which doesn't have to be repaid, and self-help aid, which can be either loans that must be repaid or work-study funds that are earned. The next sections cover the various types of financial aid that fit in one of these areas.

GRANTS

Grants typically are awarded to students who have financial needs, but they can also be awarded in the areas of athletics, academics, demographics, veteran support, and special talents. They do not have to be paid back. Grants can come from federal agencies, state agencies, specific universities, and private organizations. Most federal and state grants are based on financial need.

Examples of grants are the Pell Grant, SMART Grant, and the Federal Supplemental Educational Opportunity Grant (FSEOG). Visit the US Department of Education's Federal Student Aid site for current information about grants (see https://studentaid.ed.gov/types/grants-scholarships).

SCHOLARSHIPS

Scholarships are merit-based aid that does not have to be paid back. They are typically awarded based on academic excellence or some other special talent, such as music or art. Scholarships also fall under the areas of athletic based, minority based, aid for women, and so forth. These are typically not awarded by federal or state governments but instead come from the specific university you applied to as well as private and nonprofit organizations.

Be sure to reach out directly to the financial aid officers of the schools you want to attend. These people are great contacts who can lead you to many more sources of scholarships and financial aid. Visit http://www.gocollege.com /financial-aid/scholarships/types/ for more information about how scholarships in general work.

LOANS

Many types of loans are available especially to students to pay for their post-secondary education. However, the important thing to remember here is that loans must be paid back, with interest. Be sure you understand the interest rate you will be charged. This is the extra cost of borrowing the money and is usually a percentage of the amount you borrow. Is this fixed or will it change over time? Is the loan and interest deferred until you graduate (meaning you don't have to begin paying it off until after you graduate)? Is the loan subsidized (meaning the federal government pays the interest until you graduate)? These are all points you need to be clear about before you sign on the dotted line.

> "When we bought our first home, we purchased it because we knew we could afford it. We didn't consider the neighborhood, the location, the floor plan, or really anything besides the affordability. We realized within six months that this was not the house for us. The year was 2008, and the market tanked. We were stuck in that home for the next seven years, and it was most frustrating to be putting money into a home that we didn't feel good about. Over the years, until the market recovered, I spent many days out driving in other neighborhoods, researching homes online, and I discovered that not only was I passionate about the things that make up neighborhoods and houses, I was passionate about what a home represented."—Becks Rutledge, real estate agent

There are many types of loans offered to students, including need-based loans, non-need-based loans, state loans, and private loans. Two very reputable federal loans are the Perkins Loan and the Direct Stafford Loan. For more information about student loans, start at https://bigfuture.collegeboard.org/pay-for-college/loans/types-of-college-loans.

FEDERAL WORK-STUDY

The US Federal Work-Study Program provides part-time jobs for undergraduate and graduate students with financial need so they can earn money to pay for educational expenses. The focus of such work is on community service work and work related to a student's course of study. Not all colleges and universities participate in this program, so be sure to check with the school financial aid office if this is something you are counting on. The sooner you apply, the more likely you will get the job you desire and be able to benefit from the program, as funds are limited. See https://studentaid.ed.gov/sa/types/work-study for more information about this opportunity.

AN ENTHUSIASTIC APPROACH

Shante Johnson. *Courtesy of Shante Johnson.*

Shante Johnson brings years of experience in various aspects of the real estate industry. Her enthusiastic approach to relationship building leaves clients feeling motivated and excited about their life endeavors. As a trusted advisor with certified staging expertise, Shante effectively partners to help build her clients' dream real estate portfolios. And with her contagiously happy personality, she alleviates the stress and pains of the buying and selling process. Aside from real estate, Shante loves spending time with her family and advocating for families and coworkers of police officers killed in the line of duty.

* * *

How did you choose real estate as a career?

I was in my early twenties and was a leasing agent for a four-hundred-unit apartment community. My friend at the time was working for a builder and mentioned to me that most of the real estate agents working for the company were making six-figure incomes. They sat in beautifully decorated model homes and had nine-to-five jobs. I couldn't believe it! I was sitting in a beautiful office, showing decorated apartment homes and working the same schedule for $20K a year. It was the same thing!! I immediately enrolled in real estate school and landed a job with that builder.

Can you describe your educational background and career path to date?

I have a high school diploma and a state-issued real estate license. In Utah, where I am currently licensed, you don't need a degree to become a real estate agent. You can go into this profession straight from high school. You need to obtain 120 hours of real estate agent licensure training from a certified real estate school.

What is a typical day on the job for you?

That is the fun thing about real estate: you do many things over and over to make sure you are always lead generating (it's a contact sport), but every day can be so different. I try to follow this daily flow system to ensure I don't get too far off track: (1) Always start with gratitude! Write two thank-you notes; (2) [make] customer service calls; (3) check calendar for deadlines coming up in the next several days; (4) confirm relationship-building appointments for the day; (5) confirm and show up to any inspections for buyers (or any closings happening that day); (6) show three to four homes; (7) confirm any listing or buyer interviews; and (8) write contracts (lots of paperwork).

What is the best or most satisfying part of your job?

I know it sounds cliché, but the best part of my job is helping people achieve the "American dream." Helping them navigate one of the biggest life decisions they will ever make, it really is such an emotional roller coaster for buyers and sellers no matter how many times they may have done it. I love knowing I helped them get out of their own way and achieve a huge milestone in their journey.

What is the most challenging part or stressful part of your job?

Letting go of the fact that I cannot control the outcome, I can only control my output and true intention.

What has been the most surprising thing about your job?

I think the thing that has surprised me the most is that it truly does take time, grit, and tenacity to make real estate a true career. I have a huge sphere of influence, and even though I had been told and taught it was going to be a lot of work and take time, in the back of my mind I thought because of my sphere and contagious personality that it would be easier and faster for me to achieve my goals. Thank goodness I have great mentors, grit, and tenacity!

What kinds of qualities and personal attributes do you consider advantageous to doing your job successfully?

Integrity, personal mastery, being a problem solver, ability to connect with people and communication skills, among many others. You do not have to be good at sales or an extrovert; you just have to be human and truly want to help your people achieve their desired goals by creating value.

How do you combat burnout?

Hire help! In real estate, when you get too busy you hire people to help; that may be an assistant, a showing agent, or a listing agent. I also make sure that I am setting boundaries and not taking appointments that interfere with time I have blocked for myself or for my family. It is a constant battle of balancing time, but if you have good people/team around you it is achievable.

How do you see your own career or the real estate field in general evolving in the future?

One of the things that drew me in and continues to make me love real estate is that there are many ways to achieve financial freedom through buying, holding, and selling real estate. Real estate has always been an investment, therefore always evolving the future. I am setting myself up for financial freedom while living off the residual income of my investment properties. My children and future family will benefit from my adventures and career in real estate.

═══════════

Summary

This chapter covered aspects of college and postsecondary schooling that you'll want to consider as you move forward. Remember that finding the right fit is especially important, as it increases the chances that you'll stay in school and earn your degree as well as have an amazing experience while you're at it.

In this chapter, we discussed how to evaluate and compare your options to get the best education for the best deal. You also learned a little about scholarships and financial aid; how the SAT and ACT work, if applicable; and how to write a unique personal statement that eloquently expresses your passions.

Note: Your real estate career goals may not require a college degree, but the information given in this chapter may help you decide whether a degree is worth pursuing despite not being a minimum requirement.

Use this chapter as a jumping-off point to dig deeper into your particular area of interest. Some tidbits of wisdom to leave you with:

- Take the SAT and ACT early in your junior year so you have time to take them again. Most universities automatically accept the highest scores, while some schools do not require these test scores at all.
- Make sure that the institution you plan to attend has an accredited program in your field of study. And be sure you understand any licensure requirements and how they may change state to state, for example.
- Don't underestimate how important campus visits are, especially in the pursuit of finding the right academic fit. Come prepared to ask questions not addressed on the school website or in the literature.
- Your personal statement is a very important piece of your application that can set you apart from others. Take the time and energy needed to make it unique and compelling.
- Don't assume you can't afford a school based on the "sticker price." Many schools offer great scholarships and aid to qualified students. It doesn't hurt to apply. This advice especially applies to minorities, veterans, and students with disabilities.
- Don't lose sight of the fact that it's important to pursue a career that you enjoy, are good at, and are passionate about! You'll be a happier person if you don't.

At this point, your career goals and aspirations should be gelling. At the least, you should have a plan for finding out more information. Remember to do the research about the university, school, or degree program before you reach out and especially before you visit. Faculty and staff find students who ask challenging questions much more impressive than those who ask questions that can be answered by spending ten minutes on the school website.

In chapter 4, we go into detail about the next steps—writing a résumé and cover letter, interviewing well, follow-up communications, and more. This is information you can use to secure internships, volunteer positions, summer jobs, and more. It's not just for college grads. In fact, the sooner you can hone these communication skills, the better off you'll be in the professional world.

4

Writing Your Résumé and Interviewing

*W*ith each chapter of this book, we have narrowed the process of planning your real estate career path, from the broadest of strokes—what jobs exist within the field and what people who have those jobs actually do—to how to plan your strategy and educational approach to making your dream job a reality. In this chapter we will cover the steps involved in applying for jobs or schools: how to prepare an effective, engaging, and informative résumé and slam-dunk an interview.

> **Note:** Whatever job, school, or organization you are seeking to attend or be employed in or by, how you present yourself in person and in writing will be a major determinant in your success and should receive just as much attention as the credentials you earn and the skills you hone.

Your résumé is your opportunity to summarize your experience, training, education, and goals and attract employers or school administrators. You can think of it like this: the goal of the résumé is to land the interview, and the goal of the interview is to land the job. Even if you do not have much working experience, you can still put together a résumé that expresses your interests and goals and the activities that illustrate your competence and interest.

As well as a résumé, you will be expected to write a cover letter, which is basically your opportunity to reveal a little bit more about your passions, your motivation for a particular job or educational opportunity, and often to express more about you personally to give a potential employer a sense of who you are and what drives you. Let relevant personal characteristics come through where appropriate in this letter. You are applying for a job within a field where trustworthiness and attention to detail are paramount, as are communication skills, so you may not want to come across as a daredevil, for example.

Giving the right impression is undoubtedly important, but don't let that make you nervous. In a résumé, cover letter, or interview, you want to put forward your best but also your genuine self. Dress professionally, proofread carefully (spelling, grammar, and typographical errors will be noticed and will work against you!), but ensure you are being yourself. Authenticity is everything in a real estate career, no matter what your role.

In this chapter, we will cover all these important aspects of the job-hunting process, and by the end you will feel confident and ready to present yourself as a candidate for the job you really want.

Writing Your Résumé

Writing your first résumé can feel challenging because you have likely not yet gained a lot of experience in a professional setting, or perhaps you have but not in a real estate role. But don't fret; employers understand that you are new to the workforce or to the particular career you are seeking.

Note: The right approach is never to exaggerate or invent experience or accomplishments, but to present yourself as someone with a good work ethic and a genuine interest in the particular job or organization and to use what you can to present yourself authentically and honestly.

There are some standard elements to an effective résumé that you should be sure to include. At the top should be your name, of course, as well as email address or other contact information. Always list your experience in chronological order, beginning with your current or most recent position—or whatever experience you want to share.

If you are a recent graduate with little work experience, you might want to begin with your education. If you've been in the working world for a while, you can opt to list your education or any certifications you have at the end.

> **Note:** You may need to customize your résumé for different purposes to ensure you are not filling it with information that does not directly link to your qualifications for a particular job.

SKILLS TO INCLUDE IN A REAL ESTATE RÉSUMÉ

For the most part, writing a résumé for a real estate position is not wildly different from writing any other kind of résumé. You want to include relevant information that highlights your qualifications for the job, including any related experience and your education and training.

Most résumés are chronological: they move from your current or most recent experience or training to your earliest. This way, you can show your educational or career progression. But illustrating your skills is extremely important if you do not have a lot of work experience to highlight.

If you are moving to the real estate profession from another career or field of study, either to find part-time work on the side or just to make a change in career path entirely, then you will want to present yourself and format yourself a little differently.

You certainly do not want any degree or training you've earned nor any work experience, professional or otherwise, to go unmentioned. Employers will want to know what knowledge and experience you bring, and it's your job to show them what skills you've gained that will be applicable to a successful job in real estate.

Consider, in this case, writing what is called a function résumé, a résumé that focuses on skills rather than work or education experience directly related to real estate. The format of a function résumé is the following:

- Name and contact information (email and phone number should be sufficient).
- Title: This should match the job title you are applying for.
- Summary of applicable skills and any experience relevant to those listed in the job posting.

  - Hard skills: These are the skills directly related to the job.
  - Additional skills: Soft skills that complement the job.

- Education: Degrees or certificates or other training completed.
- Experience: Brief listing of employers, dates, and titles.
- Industry organizations you are a member of.
- Volunteer experience.

Search online for samples of such résumés and get ideas for how to structure your interests, experience, and skill sets into an attention-grabbing, career-changing résumé.

If this is your first résumé, be sure you highlight your education where you can—any courses you've taken, be it in high school or through a community college or any other place that offers training related to your job target. Also highlight any hobbies or volunteer experience you have. But be concise: one page is usually appropriate, especially for your very first résumé.

Tip: Before preparing your résumé, try to connect with a hiring professional—a human resources person or hiring manager—in a similar position or organization you are interested in. They can give you advice on what employers look for and what information to highlight on your résumé, as well as what types of interview questions you can expect.

As important as your résumé's content is the way you design and format it. You can find several samples online of résumés that you can be inspired by. At TheBalanceCareers.com, for example, you can find many templates and design ideas.[1] You want your résumé to be attractive to the eye and formatted in a way that makes the key points easy to spot and digest; according to some research, employers take an average of six seconds to review a résumé, so you don't have a lot of time to get across your experience and value.

TEN RÉSUMÉ OBJECTIVES FOR REAL ESTATE PROFESSIONALS

One of the most important sections of a résumé to get just right is the objective. The objective is a quick but effective overview of you and what you are looking for and what you bring. A solid objective means a recruiter will keep reading to learn more about you and your experience. Keep it short, and make it impactful.

The objective should be brief but to the point. It should be focused and give a sense of you as a unique applicant—you don't want it to be generic or bland—so show how creative you can be while keeping it professional. It's important to take your time and really refine your objective so you can stand out and attract employers or clients.

Here are examples of real estate résumé objectives provided by Indeed.com to help you get ideas for your own:

- Recently licensed real estate agent with in-depth knowledge of the Bay Area, looking to apply my new credentials and enthusiasm to a real estate firm.
- Hardworking real estate professional with over 10 years of experience as an agent, looking to continue helping homebuyers find the right property as a member of Coiler Real Estate.
- Seeking a real estate agent role with Primer Realty where I can use my five years of experience and customer service abilities to assist business owners in buying, selling or renting commercial properties.
- Experienced real estate agent with an investigative nature and excellent customer service skills, dedicated to finding the best properties for my clients as an agent with Baylor Real Estate.
- Looking to start my career as a licensed real estate agent at Frederick Realty, where I can uphold business standards and expand my knowledge of real estate practices.
- Technologically proficient individual with extensive knowledge of property listing resources and client management systems looking to apply my tech skills to a real estate agent position in the Rochester area.
- Out-going individual with a year of real estate experience, eager to use what I've learned about the real estate market in the Chicago area to ensure I find the best listings for real estate clientele.
- To uphold the mission statement of Edgewater Realty to assist clients in finding their forever home. Bringing with me eight years of real estate experience and a passion for helping others.
- Licensed real estate agent who helped over 20 clients buy properties within the last year, looking to apply my enthusiasm for real estate and my motivation to close deals to a competitive realty firm.
- Innovative real estate professional, seeking to apply my sales knowledge to a role where I can help clients envision how they could transform a property into their own.[2]

"Integrity, personal mastery, being a problem solver, having the ability to connect with people, and communication skills are key skills. You do not have to be good at sales or an extrovert; you just have to be human and truly want to help your people achieve their desired goals by creating value."—Shante Johnson, real estate professional

WRITING YOUR COVER LETTER

As well as your résumé, most employers will ask that you submit a cover letter. This is a one-page letter in which you express your motivation, why you are interested in the organization or position, and what skills you possess that make you the right fit. Here are some tips for writing an effective cover letter:

- As always, proofread your text carefully before submitting it.
- Be sure you have a letter that is focused on a specific job. Do not make it too general or one size fits all. Your personality and uniqueness should come through, or the recruiter or hiring manager will move on to the next application.
- Summarize why you are right for the position. Keep it relevant and specific to what the particular publication or organization is looking for in a candidate and employee.
- Keep your letter to one page whenever possible.
- Introduce yourself in a way that makes the reader want to know more about you and encourages them to review your résumé.
- Be specific about the job you are applying for. Mention the title and be sure it is correct.
- Try to find the name of the person who will receive your letter rather than keeping it nonspecific ("to whom it may concern").
- Be sure you include your contact details.
- End with a "call to action"—a request for an interview, for example.

Linking In with Impact

As well as your paper or electronic résumé, creating a LinkedIn profile is a good way to highlight your experience and promote yourself, as well as to network. Joining professional organizations and connecting with other people in your desired field are good ways to keep abreast of changes, trends, and work opportunities.

The key elements of a LinkedIn profile are your photo, your headline, and your profile summary. These are the most revealing parts of the profile and the ones employers and connections will base their impression of you on.

The photo should be carefully chosen. Remember that LinkedIn is not Facebook or Instagram; it is not the place to share a photo of you acting too casually on vacation or at a party. According to Joshua Waldman, author of *Job Searching with Social Media for Dummies*, the choice of photo should be taken seriously and be done right.[3] His tips:

- Choose a photo in which you have a nice smile.
- Dress in professional clothing.
- Ensure that the background of the photo is pleasing to the eye. According to Waldman, some colors—like green and blue—convey a feeling of trust and stability.
- Remember, it's not a mug shot. You can be creative with the angle of your photo rather than stare directly into the camera.
- Use your photo to convey some aspect of your personality.
- Focus on your face. Visitors to your profile will see only a small thumbnail image, so be sure your face takes up most of it.

Interviewing Skills

With your sparkling résumé and LinkedIn profile, you are bound to be called for an interview. This is an important stage to reach: you will have already gone through several filters—a potential employer has gotten a quick scan of your experience and has reviewed your LinkedIn profile and has made the decision to learn more about you in person.

There's no way to know ahead of time exactly what to expect in an interview, but there are many ways to prepare yourself. You can start by learning more about the person who will be interviewing you. In the same way recruiters and employers can learn about you online, you can do the same (for a business or a professional in a business). You can see if you have any education or work experience in common, or any contacts you both know. You can find out a bit about the company culture. It's perfectly acceptable and even considered proactive in a positive way to research the person with whom you'll be interviewing, such as on LinkedIn.

Preparing yourself for the types of questions you will be asked to ensure that you offer a thoughtful and meaningful response is vital to interview success. Particularly when you are applying for a job that will require you to present yourself conversationally, it is paramount that you respond in an effective, composed manner. Consider your answers carefully, and be prepared to support them with examples and anecdotes.

Here are some questions you should be prepared to be asked. It's a good idea to consider your answers carefully, without memorizing what you mean to say (as that can throw you off and will be obvious to the interviewer). Think carefully about your responses and be prepared to deliver them in a natural manner.

- Why did you decide to enter this field? What drives your passion for working in the real estate industry?

A job interview can be stressful. You can help calm your nerves and feel more confident if you prepare ahead by thinking about answers to questions you can anticipate being asked. *kate_sept2004/iStock/ Getty Images.*

- What is your educational background? What credentials have you earned?
- What experience do you have relating to this job?
- Are you a team player? Describe your usual role in a team-centered work environment. Do you easily assume a leadership role?

BEWARE WHAT YOU SHARE ON SOCIAL MEDIA

Most of us engage in social media. Sites such as Facebook, Twitter, and Instagram provide us a platform for sharing photos and memories, opinions, and life events, and reveal everything from our political stance to our sense of humor. It's a great way to connect with people around the world, but once you post something, it's accessible to anyone—including potential employers—unless you take mindful precaution.

Your posts may be public, which means you may be making the wrong impression without realizing it. More and more, people are using search engines like Google to get a sense of potential employers, colleagues, or employees, and the impression you make online can have a strong impact on how you are perceived. Approximately 70 percent of employers search for information on candidates on social media sites.[4]

Glassdoor.com offers the following tips for how to keep your social media activity from sabotaging your career success:[5]

Check your privacy settings. Ensure that your photos and posts are only accessible to the friends or contacts you want to see them. You want to come across as professional and reliable.

Rather than avoid social media while searching for a job, use it to your advantage. It's to your advantage to have an online presence (as long as it's a flattering one). Give future employers a sense of your professional interest by "liking" pages or joining groups of professional organizations related to your career goals.

Grammar counts. Be attentive to the quality of writing of all your posts and comments.

Be consistent. With each social media outlet, there is a different focus and tone of what you are communicating. LinkedIn is very professional while Facebook is far more social and relaxed. It's okay to take a different tone on various social media sites, but be sure you aren't blatantly contradicting yourself.

Choose your username carefully. Remember, social media may be the first impression anyone has of you in the professional realm.

DRESSING APPROPRIATELY

How you dress for a job interview is very important to the impression you want to make. Remember that the interview, no matter what the actual environment in which you'd be working, is your chance to present your most professional self. Although you will not likely ever wear a suit to work, for the interview it's the most professional choice.

> **Tip:** For real estate professionals, the image you project is very important. While you may not need to wear a suit to an interview, it would be a mistake to dress too casually. Clients especially will look to you for professionalism when choosing you to represent them, so employers will definitely be looking for you to appear dressed the part.

WHAT EMPLOYERS EXPECT

Hiring managers and human resources professionals will also have certain expectations of you at an interview. The main thing is preparation: it cannot be overstated that you should arrive to an interview appropriately dressed, on time, unhurried, and ready to answer—and ask—questions. For any job interview, these are the main things you should do:

- Have a thorough understanding of the organization and the job for which you are applying.
- Be prepared to answer questions about yourself and your relevant experience.
- Be poised and likeable, but still professional. Employers will be looking for a sense of what it would be like to work with you on a daily basis and how your presence would fit in the culture of the business.
- Stay engaged. Listen carefully to what is being asked and offer thoughtful but concise answers. Don't blurt out answers you've memorized, but really focus on what is being asked.

- Be prepared to ask your own questions. It shows how much you understand the flow of an organization or workplace and how you will contribute to it. Some questions you can ask:

  - What created the need to fill this position? Is it a new position or has someone left the organization?
  - Where does this position fit in the overall hierarchy of the organization?
  - What are the key skills required to succeed in this job?
  - What challenges might I expect to face within the first six months on the job?
  - How does this position relate to the achievement of the organization's (or department's, or boss's) goals?
  - How would you describe the organization's culture?

You may find yourself interviewing virtually, using technology such as Zoom, rather than appearing in person. This is almost certainly the case during the time of the pandemic, but it may also be your circumstance if you are applying to a job far away from where you live.

To prepare for an online interview, you should follow the same preparation tips as you would for an in-person meeting, but be sure to test the technology ahead of time (including any applications you need to use, passwords you require, microphone, camera, and so on). You can also test to see how your outfit or background appears to the person with whom you will be meeting. There is nothing worse than discovering your interviewer can't hear you properly or that there is anything unprofessional or inappropriate visible to the interviewer.

LIVING AND LOVING REAL ESTATE

Becks Rutledge was born and raised in Iowa, moved six times in two years, then found herself living and loving life in Salt Lake City, Utah. She is a mother of three children, a real estate agent, a lover of all things outdoors, and a self-proclaimed book junkie. Becks enjoys exploring all facets of real estate, which is not just buying and selling homes; it includes so much more, and she loves every minute of it. The motto "When you love what you do, you'll never work a day in your life" is exactly Becks and her path.

Becks Rutledge. *Courtesy of Becks Rutledge.*

* * *

How did you choose real estate as a career?

When we bought our first home, we purchased it because we knew we could afford it. We didn't consider the neighborhood, the location, the floor plan, or really anything besides the affordability. We realized within six months that this was not the house for us. The year was 2008, and the market tanked. We were stuck in that home for the next seven years, and it was most frustrating to be putting money into a home that we didn't feel good about. Over the years, until the market recovered, I spent many days out driving in other neighborhoods, researching homes online, and I discovered that not only was I passionate about the things that make up neighborhoods and houses, I was passionate about what a home represented.

Can you describe your educational background and career path to date?

I originally went to college for elementary education, and quickly discovered that was not the direction for me. I have always loved the medical field and actually was in radiology, but after having time off and being a mom for a few years as we moved around, that's when I really dug into real estate and it's been the best decision.

What is a typical day on the job for you?

I am an independent contractor, which means I can come and go as I please. I work for myself, and while I enjoy all of those aspects, I treat my job like a nine-to-five. You get back everything you put into it and then some. I show up, am constantly on my phone, my emails, and in my car. It's not exactly a desk job, but if you don't have any business going, it means you need to be making calls, mentioning your work on social media, connecting with past clients, and knowing exactly what is happening in the market.

What's the best or most satisfying part of your job?

All of it. I love every second. Being able to involve my kids, take them with me to show houses, work from home if needed is a good start. I also love helping my clients. It is exciting to walk them through houses and hear them talk about what they would do with this room, or how they would enjoy the space. Watching them dream and then making that dream come to life, yes . . . that's the best part.

What's the most challenging part or stressful part of your job?

Negotiations are the most stressful. I'm not a bulldog at heart, but I learned early on that it's most important that your client feels heard and understood, all while making sure that we make the negotiations as smooth as possible. I always want it to feel like a win for both parties.

What has been the most surprising thing about your job?

The most surprising thing has been finding out that real estate can take on so many more avenues than just residential. I work with a team that has a good focus on residential business, but we also represent buyers and sellers in commercial transactions, as well as investors who look for rentals, multi-unit homes, and Airbnb.

What kinds of qualities and personal attributes do you consider advantageous to doing your job successfully?

I am a people person, 100 percent. It's important that people in real estate not only are enjoyable to be around, [but also] that they can continue to learn and understand the market they are working in. They need to be driven and self-motivated.

How do you combat burnout?

This is a career that truly is a life by design. You make it what you want it. I don't get burned out because I design my day and my life around it. I journal every morning about my goals and it's exciting to watch these moments unfold. I always make sure to take time for myself, and I've learned that it's okay to put down your phone, close out your email, and enjoy moments.

How do you see your own career or the real estate field in general evolving in the future?

I see my career only continuing to grow. This is only the beginning for me, and by that I mean continuing to help others buy and sell, but also I will invest in properties myself to grow in the field as an investor. The brokerage I am with focuses on a life worth living and a legacy worth leaving.

═══════════

Summary

Congratulations on working through the book! You should now have a strong idea of your career goals within the real estate field, and how to realize them. In this chapter, we covered how to present yourself as the right candidate to a potential employer—and these strategies are also relevant if you are applying to a college or another form of training. Here are some tips to sum it up:

- Your résumé should be concise and focused on only relevant aspects of your work experience or education. Although you can include some personal hobbies or details, they should be related to the job and your qualifications for it.
- Take your time with all your professional documents—your résumé, your cover letter, your LinkedIn profile—and be sure to proofread very carefully to avoid embarrassing and sloppy mistakes.
- Prepare yourself for an interview, anticipating the types of questions you will be asked and coming up with professional and meaningful responses.
- Equally, prepare some questions to ask to your potential employer at the interview. This will show you have a good understanding and interest in the organization and what role you would have in it.
- Always follow up after an interview with a letter or an email. An email is the fastest way to express your gratitude for the interviewer's time and restate your interest in the position.
- Dress appropriately for an interview and pay extra attention to tidiness and hygiene.

- Be wary of what you share on social media sites while job searching. Most employers research candidates online, and what you have shared will influence their idea of who you are and what it would be like to work with you.

You've chosen to pursue a career in a competitive, challenging, but also broad and exciting field. I wish you great success in your future.

Appendix

Additional Resources

The following websites, publications, and organizations can help you further investigate and educate yourself on real estate profession–related topics, all of which will help you as you take the next steps in your career, now and throughout your professional life.

Publications

URBAN LAND

The magazine of the Urban Land Institute (ULI). It is published in print editions per year, but online articles are published nearly every business day. https://urbanland.uli.org.

AREA DEVELOPMENT

A resource that provides insights and information that ensure success for expanding companies and their advisors when considering new facility locations. https://www.areadevelopment.com/.

COMMERCIAL MORTGAGE INSIGHT

A monthly journal for the top professionals in commercial mortgage finance, including mortgage bankers, commercial banks, and community/savings institutions involved with commercial and multifamily mortgages. https://www.socialworker.com/magazine.

REALTOR MAGAZINE

The official magazine of the National Association of Realtors and the business tool for real estate professionals. https://magazine.realtor/.

REALTY 411 MAGAZINE

Features commentary, information about tools and companies, and interviews with leaders in the property investment industry. http://realty411guide.com/.

Organizations

THE AMERICAN GUILD OF APPRAISERS

An association of professional real estate appraisers formed to promote appraiser independence, the maintenance of high-level professional standards in real estate appraisal practice, and the use of professional appraisers to protect the public interest. https://www.appraisersguild.org/.

COMMERCIAL REAL ESTATE DEVELOPMENT ASSOCIATION

An organization for developers, owners, and related professionals in office, industrial, and mixed-use real estate. NAIOP comprises more than eighteen thousand members in North America and advocates for both responsible commercial real estate development and effective public policy. https://www.naiop.org/.

NATIONAL ASSOCIATION OF REALTORS

The largest trade association in the US, representing 1.5 million members, including NAR's institutes, societies, and councils, involved in all aspects of the residential and commercial real estate industries. https://www.nar.realtor/.

AMERICAN REAL ESTATE SOCIETY

An association of real estate thought leaders. Members come from academic and professional sectors, both in the US and internationally. The society is

dedicated to producing and sharing knowledge related to real estate decision-making and the functioning of real estate markets. https://www.ares
net.org/.

ASSOCIATION OF INDEPENDENT MORTGAGE EXPERTS

A nonprofit, national trade membership association created for independent
mortgage brokers. https://aimegroup.com/.

NATIONAL ASSOCIATION OF REAL ESTATE ADVISORS

An organization that strives to help real estate professionals boost their learning
and income potential, by providing exceptional education through its designa-
tion programs, as well as facilitating networking and knowledge sharing among
its members. https://nareagroup.org/.

NATIONAL ASSOCIATION OF RESIDENTIAL PROPERTY MANAGERS

An association of real estate professionals who understand and can help navigate the unique problems and challenges of managing single-family and small
residential properties. https://www.narpm.org/.

NATIONAL ASSOCIATION OF BROKER PRICE OPINION PROFESSIONALS

A nonprofit trade association composed of broker price opinion (BPO) prac-
titioners (real estate brokers and sales agents) from across the country. https://
nabpop.org/.

INTERNATIONAL COUNCIL OF SHOPPING CENTERS

A member organization that promotes and elevates the marketplaces and spaces
where people shop, dine, work, play, and gather as foundational and vital ingre-
dients of communities and economies. https://www.icsc.com/.

Websites

WWW.ZILLOW.COM

Founded in 2006 by two former Microsoft executives, Zillow offers a robust suite of tools for buyers, sellers, landlords, renters, agents, and other home professionals.

WWW.REALTOR.COM

Affiliated with the National Association of Realtors and linked to more than 580 regional Multiple Listing Services, this site includes prime listings and is updated regularly by Realtors.

WWW.TRULIA.COM

Founded in 2005, Trulia is both a website and mobile app that prides itself on the transparency it offers potential home buyers and renters who use it to search for properties.

WWW.FORECLOSURE.COM

There are several real estate websites dedicated to foreclosures, but Foreclosure.com has a mix of search criteria, sorting, quantity of listings, and, perhaps most importantly with this complex process, education.

WWW.APARTMENTS.COM

This site offers renters information not only about their apartment choices but also about the surrounding community and tips on improving their rental experience.

Notes

Introduction

1. National Association of Realtors, "Quick Real Estate Statistics," November 11, 2020, accessed November 16, 2021, https://www.nar.realtor/research-and-statistics/quick-real-estate-statistics.

2. Bureau of Labor Statistics, "Real Estate Brokers and Sales Agents," accessed November 16, 2021, https://www.bls.gov/ooh/sales/real-estate-brokers-and-sales-agents.htm.

3. UpNest, "Is Job Security Something Real Estate Agents Need to Worry About?," October 13, 2021, accessed November 16, 2021, https://www.upnest.com/1/post/future-of-real-estate-how-safe-are-real-estate-agent-jobs/.

4. UpNest, "Job Security."

Chapter 1

1. Bureau of Labor Statistics, "Real Estate Brokers and Sales Agents," accessed November 17, 2021, https://www.bls.gov/ooh/sales/real-estate-brokers-and-sales-agents.htm.

2. Bureau of Labor Statistics, "Real Estate Brokers and Sales Agents."

3. Salary.com, "Real Estate Assistant Salary in the United States," accessed November 17, 2021, https://www.salary.com/research/salary/posting/real-estate-assistant-salary.

4. Bureau of Labor Statistics, "Real Estate Brokers and Sales Agents."

5. Bureau of Labor Statistics, "Property, Real Estate, and Community Association Managers," accessed November 17, 2021, https://www.bls.gov/ooh/management/property-real-estate-and-community-association-managers.htm.

6. Corporate Finance Institute, "Real Estate," accessed November 17, 2021, https://corporatefinanceinstitute.com/resources/careers/jobs/real-estate/.

7. Marco Santarelli, "Housing Market Predictions 2022: Will it Crash or Boom?," accessed July 20, 2022, https://www.noradarealestate.com/blog/housing -market-predictions/.

Chapter 2

1. Kaplan Real Estate Education, "Is a Career as a Real Estate Broker Right for You?," August 8, 2019, accessed November 18, 2021, https://www.kapre.com /resources/real-estate/is-a-career-as-a-real-estate-broker-right-for-you/.

2. Jane E. Shersher, "Self Care Tips for Social Workers," SocialWorkLicensure .org, accessed April 21, 2021, https://socialworklicensure.org/articles/self-care-tips/.

3. Eman Hamed, "How to Become a Property Manager in 5 Steps," Mashvisor. com, June 11, 2019, accessed November 18, 2021, https://www.mashvisor.com/blog /how-to-become-a-property-manager-5-steps/.

4. AllPropertyManagement.com, "Property Management Laws by State," accessed November 18, 2021, https://www.allpropertymanagement.com/resources /property-management-laws/.

Chapter 3

1. Steven R. Antonoff, "College Personality Quiz," *U.S. News & World Report*, July 31, 2018, accessed May 21, 2021, https://www.usnews.com/education/best-col leges/right-school/choices/articles/college-personality-quiz.

2. Alex Gailey, "Taking a Gap Year during Coronavirus? Here's How to Make the Most of It," NextAdvisor, September 29, 2020, accessed May 21, 2021, https:// time.com/nextadvisor/in-the-news/gap-year-coronavirus/.

3. Claudia Hammond, "Does Reading Fiction Make Us Better People?," BBC .com, June 3, 2019, accessed March 2, 2021, https://www.bbc.com/future/article /20190523-does-reading-fiction-make-us-better-people.

4. FairTest, "1,425+ Accredited, 4-Year Colleges & Universities with ACT/ SAT-Optional Testing Policies for Fall, 2022 Admissions," updated May 17, 2021, accessed May 21, 2021, https://fairtest.org/university/optional.

5. *U.S. News & World Report*, "Best Undergraduate Real Estate Programs," accessed November 19, 2021, https://www.usnews.com/best-colleges/rankings/business-real-estate?_ga=2.129753356.1261472458.1637168787-251120869.1637065102.

6. Farran Powell and Emma Kerr, "See the Average College Tuition in 2020–2021," *U.S. News & World Report*, September 14, 2020, accessed May 2, 2021, https://www.usnews.com/education/best-colleges/paying-for-college/articles/paying-for-college-infographic.

7. Powell and Kerr, "Average College Tuition."

8. Emma Kerr, "How Colleges Are Adjusting Their 2021–2022 Tuition," *U.S. News & World Report*, January 21, 2021, accessed May 2, 2021, https://www.usnews.com/education/best-colleges/paying-for-college/articles/how-colleges-are-adjusting-their-2021-2022-tuition.

Chapter 4

1. Alison Doyle, "Student Resume Examples, Templates, and Writing Tips," TheBalanceCareers.com, accessed May 21, 2021, https://www.thebalancecareers.com/student-resume-examples-and-templates-2063555.

2. Indeed.com, "Real Estate Resume Objectives: Tips and 20 Examples," February 23, 2021, accessed November 22, 2021, https://www.indeed.com/career-advice/resumes-cover-letters/resume-objective-real-estate.

3. Joshua Waldman, *Job Searching with Social Media for Dummies* (Hoboken, NJ: Wiley, 2013).

4. SecurityMagazine.com, "70 Percent of Employers Check Candidates' Social Media Profiles," September 23, 2018, accessed May 21, 2021, https://www.securitymagazine.com/gdpr-policy?url=https%3A%2F%2Fwww.securitymagazine.com%2Farticles%2F89441-percent-of-employers-check-candidates-social-media-profiles.

5. Alice A. M. Underwood, "9 Things to Avoid on Social Media while Looking for a New Job," Glassdoor, January 3, 2018, accessed October 30, 2020, https://www.glassdoor.com/blog/things-to-avoid-on-social-media-job-search/.

Glossary

bachelor's degree. A four-year degree awarded by a college or university.

background check. A process a person or company uses to verify that a person is who they claim to be.

burnout. Feeling of physical and emotional exhaustion caused by overworking.

campus. The location of a school, college, or university.

career assessment test. A test that asks questions particularly geared to identify skills and interests to help inform the test taker on what type of career would suit them.

colleagues. The people with whom you work.

commercial property. Commercial property refers to land and buildings that are used by businesses to carry out their operations. Examples include shopping malls, individual stores, office buildings, parking lots, medical centers, and hotels.

community college. A two-year college that awards associate's degrees.

cover letter. A document that usually accompanies a résumé and allows a candidate applying to a job, school, or internship an opportunity to describe their motivation and qualifications.

educational background. The degrees a person has earned and schools attended.

empathy. The quality of being able to understand the feelings of another person.

entrepreneur. A person who works for themselves and operates their own business, big or small.

entry level. A position in a career usually held by a person who is just starting out in their professional life, with their first professional job. Usually this indicates a lower salary and level of responsibility to start than jobs held by more experienced workers.

ethics. Moral principles that govern a person's behavior or the conducting of an activity.

financial aid. Various means of receiving financial support for the purposes of attending school. This can be a grant or scholarship, for example.

gap year. A year between high school and higher education or employment during which a person can explore their passions and interests, often while traveling.

industrial property. Industrial real estate is a type of property used by businesses for activities such as factory work, mechanical productions, research and development, construction, transportation, logistics, and warehousing.

industry. The people and activities involved in one type of business, such as the business of real estate.

in-state school. A nonprivate college that exists in the state in which you are a resident. In-state schools offer lower tuitions to state residents.

internship. A work experience opportunity that lasts for a set period of time and can be paid or unpaid.

interpersonal skills. The ability to communicate and interact with other people in an effective manner.

interviewing. A part of the job-seeking process in which a candidate meets with a potential employer, usually face-to-face, to discuss their work experience and education and seek information about the position.

job market. A market in which employers search for employees and employees search for jobs.

land (in real estate). Land is often not thought of as real estate because it mostly is not valued for any buildings or structures, but for the space itself. It is the starting point for all types of real property. Developers purchase land with plans to use it for a specific, designed purpose, such as an office park or housing area.

license. A proof of a qualification earned by passing a state-administered test, or a test administered by any other official party.

major. The subject or course of study in which you choose to earn your degree.

master's degree. A degree that is sought by those who have already earned a bachelor's degree in order to further their education.

mortgage. A particular type of loan one takes from a bank particularly for buying property.

neighborhood. A particular district or community within a town or city.

networking. The processes of building, strengthening, and maintaining professional relationships as a way to further your career goals.

out-of-state school. A nonprivate college that exists in a state other than in which you are a resident. These schools have higher tuitions for those who are not residents of that state.

real estate agents. They help clients buy and sell properties, as well as rent or rent out properties.

real estate appraisers. They estimate the value of the property before the property is sold, taxed, mortgaged, or insured. This requires additional licensure.

real estate brokers. They are responsible for negotiations between buyer and seller parties and for arranging real estate transactions.

real estate development. A process that involves the purchase of raw land, rezoning, construction and renovation of buildings, and sale or lease of the finished product to end users.

real estate marketing specialists. They create marketing content, manage social media, develop printed materials, create digital content, prepare campaign emails, and manage the brand as a whole for real estate agencies.

real estate property managers. They take care of a property, both financially and in terms of maintenance, and see to the needs of any tenants living or working there.

real estate transaction coordinators. They serve as a liaison between the client, real estate agent, escrow company, and mortgage brokers.

Realtor. A real estate agent who is also a member of the National Association of Realtors, the largest trade association in the US.

residential property. Residential real estate is something we are all familiar with: the structures in which people live. This can mean single-family homes, apartments, condominiums, townhouses, and other types of living spaces.

résumé. A document, usually one page, that outlines a candidate's professional experience and education and that is designed to give potential employers a sense of that person's qualifications.

showing assistants. They assist agents by presenting a property to clients and telling them all about it.

social media. Websites and applications that enable users to create and share content online for networking and social-sharing purposes. Examples include Facebook, LinkedIn, Twitter, and Instagram.

tuition. The money you have to pay for education, be it a college or university degree or a certification.

work culture. A concept that defines the beliefs, philosophy, thought processes, and attitudes of employees in a particular organization.

Bibliography

AllPropertyManagement.com. "Property Management Laws by State." Accessed November 18, 2021. https://www.allpropertymanagement.com/resources/property-management-laws/.

Antonoff, Steven R. "College Personality Quiz." *U.S. News & World Report.* July 31, 2018. Accessed May 21, 2021. https://www.usnews.com/education/best-colleges/right-school/choices/articles/college-personality-quiz.

Bureau of Labor Statistics. "Property, Real Estate, and Community Association Managers." Accessed November 17, 2021. https://www.bls.gov/ooh/management/property-real-estate-and-community-association-managers.htm.

———. "Real Estate Brokers and Sales Agents." Accessed November 16, 2021. https://www.bls.gov/ooh/sales/real-estate-brokers-and-sales-agents.htm.

Corporate Finance Institute. "Real Estate." Accessed November 17, 2021. https://corporatefinanceinstitute.com/resources/careers/jobs/real-estate/.

Doyle, Alison. "Student Resume Examples, Templates, and Writing Tips." The BalanceCareers.com. Accessed May 21, 2021. https://www.thebalancecareers.com/student-resume-examples-and-templates-2063555.

FairTest. "1,425+ Accredited, 4-Year Colleges & Universities with ACT/SAT-Optional Testing Policies for Fall, 2022 Admissions." Updated May 17, 2021. Accessed May 21, 2021. https://fairtest.org/university/optional.

Gailey, Alex. "Taking a Gap Year during Coronavirus? Here's How to Make the Most of It." NextAdvisor. September 29, 2020. Accessed May 21, 2021. https://time.com/nextadvisor/in-the-news/gap-year-coronavirus/.

Hamed, Eman. "How to Become a Property Manager in 5 Steps." Mashvisor.com. June 11, 2019. Accessed November 18, 2021. https://www.mashvisor.com/blog/how-to-become-a-property-manager-5-steps/.

Hammond, Claudia. "Does Reading Fiction Make Us Better People?" BBC.com. June 3, 2019. Accessed March 2, 2021. https://www.bbc.com/future/article/20190523-does-reading-fiction-make-us-better-people.

Indeed.com. "Real Estate Resume Objectives: Tips and 20 Examples." February 23, 2021. Accessed November 22, 2021. https://www.indeed.com/career-advice/resumes-cover-letters/resume-objective-real-estate.

Kaplan Real Estate Education. "Is a Career as a Real Estate Broker Right for You?" August 8, 2019. Accessed November 18, 2021. https://www.kapre.com/resources/real-estate/is-a-career-as-a-real-estate-broker-right-for-you/.

Kerr, Emma. "How Colleges Are Adjusting Their 2021–2022 Tuition." *U.S. News & World Report.* January 21, 2021. Accessed May 2, 2021. https://www.usnews.com/education/best-colleges/paying-for-college/articles/how-colleges-are-adjusting-their-2021-2022-tuition.

National Association of Realtors. "Quick Real Estate Statistics." November 11, 2020. Accessed November 16, 2021. https://www.nar.realtor/research-and-statistics/quick-real-estate-statistics.

Powell, Farran, and Emma Kerr. "See the Average College Tuition in 2020–2021." *U.S. News & World Report.* September 14, 2020. Accessed May 2, 2021. https://www.usnews.com/education/best-colleges/paying-for-college/articles/paying-for-college-infographic.

Salary.com. "Real Estate Assistant Salary in the United States." Accessed November 17, 2021. https://www.salary.com/research/salary/posting/real-estate-assistant-salary.

Santarelli, Marco. "Housing Market Predictions 2022: Will it Crash or Boom?" Accessed July 20, 2022. https://www.noradarealestate.com/blog/housing-market-predictions/.

SecurityMagazine.com. "70 Percent of Employers Check Candidates' Social Media Profiles." September 23, 2018. Accessed May 21, 2021. https://www.securitymagazine.com/gdpr-policy?url=https%3A%2F%2Fwww.securitymagazine.com%2Farticles%2F89441-percent-of-employers-check-candidates-social-media-profiles.

Shersher, Jane E. "Self Care Tips for Social Workers." SocialWorkLicensure.org. Accessed April 21, 2021. https://socialworklicensure.org/articles/self-care-tips/.

Underwood, Alice A. M. "9 Things to Avoid on Social Media while Looking for a New Job." Glassdoor. January 3, 2018. Accessed October 30, 2020. https://www.glassdoor.com/blog/things-to-avoid-on-social-media-job-search/.

UpNest. "Is Job Security Something Real Estate Agents Need to Worry About?"
October 13, 2021. Accessed November 16, 2021. https://www.upnest
.com/1/post/future-of-real-estate-how-safe-are-real-estate-agent-jobs/.

U.S. News & World Report. "Best Undergraduate Real Estate Programs." Accessed
November 19, 2021. https://www.usnews.com/best-colleges/rankings
/business-real-estate?_ga=2.129753356.1261472458.1637168787-2511
20869.1637065102.

Waldman, Joshua. *Job Searching with Social Media for Dummies.* Hoboken, NJ:
Wiley, 2013.

About the Author

Tracy Brown Hamilton is a writer, editor, and journalist based in the Netherlands. She has written several books on topics ranging from careers to media, economics to pop culture. She lives with her husband and three children.